WEST E...

Heroes of Jewish History

ABRAHAM TO MOSES

Damascus
To Babylon
Sea of Galilee
Bashan
Mt. Carmel
MEDITERRANEAN SEA
Jordon
Gilead
Shechem
Jaffa
Jericho
Mt. Nebo
Bethel
Jerusalem
Sodom
Bethlehem
Hebron
Moab
Dead Sea
Gaza
Beersheba
Negev
Edom
Kadesh
To Egypt
Midian
Desert of Paran
C.E.P.
To Arabia
THE LAND OF ISRAEL
Mt. Sinai
Red Sea

HEROES OF JEWISH HISTORY

From Abraham to Moses

WITH EXERCISES
PROJECTS AND GAMES

By

MORDECAI H. LEWITTES

Illustrations by
AUDREY NAMOWITZ

HEBREW PUBLISHING COMPANY
NEW YORK

Copyright 1952
by Hebrew Publishing Company, New York
Printed in the United States of America

PRINTED AND BOUND IN U. S. A. BY
MONTAUK BOOK MANUFACTURING CO., INC., NEW YORK

TO HEDVA JANE
AND TO HER FRIENDS EVERYWHERE
WHO WANT TO LEARN THE STORY
OF THEIR PEOPLE

Preface

Educators have long felt that the story of the heroes of our people can best serve as an introduction to Jewish history. Ben Sira well understood this when he wrote, "And the praise of men of fame and the glory of our ancestors I shall recite—each man in his generation."

Which child does not thrill to hear the tale of the heroes of old? The dramatic narratives of the Bible, in particular, lend themselves to retelling. A text which omits these stories is almost like the proverbial presentation of Hamlet without the prince.

The mere story, of course, is not enough. The author has sought to provide a brief description of the historical background, as in the opening chapter about the city of Ur, birthplace of Abraham. The holidays, which present such an excellent point of contact with modern Jewish life, have been emphasized throughout the book. There is a clear analysis—on the child's level of understanding—of the significance of each major personality.

But, above all, there must be a challenge to the pupil. Through varied exercises and projects the child is stimulated to think about what he has read, and to give concrete form to his ideas. The thought questions, included after each chapter, can serve as the focal point for fruitful classroom discussions. Play, too, has an important place in the school, and the many games and puzzles found in the book will prove to be a source of fun.

Other pedagogic aids, such as maps, illustrations, review material, tests and pronunciation guide will also be helpful to teacher and pupil. The resourceful instructor, of course, will not follow any text slavishly, but will adapt the printed material in keeping with the special needs and interests of his students.

The author sincerely hopes that this volume will instill in the child a love for the study of Jewish history. We have been called "the people of the book", for a knowledge of the past is indispensable to Jews. It is not only the key to our understanding of our rich heritage, but the basis for a living, dynamic Judaism in our own day.

Contents

PAGE

UNIT ONE
Abraham, the Father of the Hebrew People

1.	In the City of Ur	15
2.	Abraham in the Promised Land	23
3.	The Destruction of Sodom	32

UNIT TWO
The Children of Abraham

4.	Ishmael and Isaac	45
5.	The Story of Isaac	52
6.	The Beautiful Rebecca	59

UNIT THREE
Jacob

7.	Jacob and Esau	71
8.	Jacob in Haran	79
9.	Jacob's Return to Canaan	87

UNIT FOUR
Joseph and His Brothers

10.	Joseph the Dreamer	97
11.	From Prison to Prime Minister	103
12.	Joseph and Benjamin	111
13.	Reunion in Egypt	120

PAGE

UNIT FIVE
Out of the House of Bondage

14.	Moses	129
15.	"Let My People Go"	138
16.	The Ten Plagues	145
17.	The Holiday of Passover	153

UNIT SIX
In the Wilderness

18.	At Sinai	165
19.	After Sinai	174
20.	Rebellion	180
21.	Near the Land of Canaan	189
22.	The Last Days of Moses	197
	Glossary	205

Illustrations

	PAGE
The Land of Israel	*Frontispiece*
Abraham Praying for Sodom	33
Around the Campfire	53
Rebecca and Isaac	63
Jacob the Shepherd	83
Joseph and His Brothers	115
Pharaoh's Daughter and Moses	131
Slaves in Egypt	147
The Seder	157
Moses and the Ten Commandments	169
The Fruits of Canaan	181

UNIT ONE

Abraham, the Father of the Hebrew People

CHAPTER I

IN THE CITY OF UR

1. THE BELIEF IN ONE GOD

ABRAHAM was the first Hebrew.
He was born long, long ago in a city named Ur. There he lived with his father, his mother and his two small brothers.

In those days nobody knew about God. In the city of Ur stood a large temple which looked like the tower of Babel. This temple was built in honor of the moon, for the people thought that the moon was god.

Often the king and all the men and women of Ur would gather to worship the moon. Once Abraham's father called to Abraham and said, "My son, let us go to the temple to-night to worship the moon-god."

"I shall be ready, my father," said Abraham.

This was the first time that Abraham had joined in the worship of the moon, and he waited eagerly for the hour when he and his father would depart from their home.

There was a full moon that night, and to Abraham it looked like a silver ship as it floated through the heavens.

Abraham took the flour and placed it in front of the largest idol.

"Now I can prove to everybody that idols are not real," said Abraham to himself.

Quickly he threw all the idols, except the largest one, to the ground. There was a loud crash as each idol fell to the floor. Abraham then took a hammer and placed it in the hand of the large idol.

When Terah returned he found the broken idols.

"Who did this?" asked Terah in an angry voice.

"The large idol," answered Abraham.

"What do you mean?" shouted Terah.

"The idols began to argue about the flour," replied Abraham. "Each idol wanted the flour for himself. At last the large idol took a hammer and destroyed the other idols."

"But that is impossible," said Terah. "Idols cannot move, or argue, or strike each other. They are made of only wood or clay."

"If so," said Abraham, "why do you bow down to statues of wood and of clay? And why do you worship these idols? God made the heavens and the earth, and only Him must we worship."

Terah saw that his son spoke the truth, and he too began to believe in God.

3. ABRAHAM'S FAMILY LEAVES UR

As Abraham grew older he learned many things. Wise men in Ur already knew how to write. They used picture-writing. They did not write on paper. Instead they wrote on clay tablets.

Through these tablets Abraham learned the history of Ur. He learned that once there had been a flood which covered the entire land beneath its waters.

Ur was then the largest city in the world. In other cities stood houses made of mud, but in Ur there were fine houses made of burnt brick. In these houses were cups and vessels made of silver and gold, for the goldsmiths of Ur were the best in the world.

Ur rested along the banks of the Euphrates River. The kings of Ur built canals so that boats could sail from Ur to the Persian Gulf. These sailboats brought back to Ur food and clothing and precious stones.

When Abraham grew up he married a beautiful girl named Sarah. She too began to believe in one God. Sarah is called "the mother of the Hebrew people."

One day Terah called Abraham and the other members of the family together. "My children," he said, "the time has come for us to leave Ur."

"But why must we leave?" asked Abraham's brother. "Ur is a rich city, and its boats bring us good things from all the lands of the world."

"It is no longer so, my son," replied Terah. "The king does not take care of the city as did the kings before him. He either goes hunting or wages war. The canals lie in ruins. Boats find it hard to reach the sea. The sands of the desert are at our very doorstep."

The sand was Ur's greatest enemy. The desert sandstorms grew stronger and stronger from year to year. Sometimes the wind would blow with such force that the sand would enter one's mouth, and eyes and nostrils. It was hard to breathe, and it would get so dark that one could hardly see his own hand.

Abraham agreed to leave. He knew that the king of Ur was angry because Abraham would not bow down to idols. Maybe they would find a city where people would listen to his words about God.

Terah and his family placed all their goods on camels and on donkeys, and began to move northward. They took the path near the Euphrates River that led past the great city of Babylon. But they did not stop here.

On and on they went. At last they came to a city in the Land of the Two Rivers called Haran.

"Here we will make our home," said Terah.

Terah and his family pitched their tents near Haran. Their sheep grazed in the green fields outside of Haran near the Euphrates River.

And many people in Haran heard of the wisdom of Abraham and Sarah. They began to believe in one God, and would no longer worship the moon or bow down to idols.

Terah's words about Ur came true. Because of war the canals and houses were ruined and the city became poorer and poorer. After many, many years the sands of the desert covered the houses, and the world forgot about Ur.

Some years ago an American college sent scientists to

Ur to clear away the sand. They hired hundreds of Arabs, and dug, and dug, and dug until they found the hidden city of Ur. They found the king's palace, and the temple to the moon-god, and brick houses and golden helmets and daggers. They even found signs of the flood that once covered Ur.

And so once more the world has learned about Ur, the great city in which Abraham was born.

EXERCISES

I. Fill in the correct name—Abraham or Terah. (Review section 1, pages 15 to 17.)
1. _____ was the father of 3 sons.
2. _____ was the first Hebrew.
3. _____ believed in the moon-god.
4. _____ believed in one God.

II. True or false? (Review section 2, pages 17 to 18.)
1. The man bought an idol.
2. The woman brought a dish of flour.
3. Abraham placed the flour in front of the large idol.
4. The large idol broke the small idols.
5. Abraham wanted to prove that idols are not real.

III. Select the correct word. (Review section 3, pages 18 to 21.)
1. Abraham was born in _____. (Ur, Jerusalem)
2. Ur was near the _____ River. (Euphrates, Jordan)
3. Ur had many _____. (blacksmiths, goldsmiths)

4. People in Ur wrote on _____. (paper, clay)
5. Terah moved to _____. (Babylon, Haran)

IV. Questions for discussion:
1. Compare Ur with the city in which you live.
2. Why isn't Noah called the father of the Hebrew people?

THINGS TO DO

1. *A Play*—Act out the legend of Abraham and the broken idols. The following parts are needed: the story-teller, Abraham, the man, the woman, Terah.
2. *Art Work*—Draw one of these pictures: Terah and Abraham; the sailboats of Ur; Abraham taking care of the sheep at Haran.
3. *Story Hour*—Arrange a Bible story hour. Tell one of these stories: Adam and Eve, Cain and Abel, Noah and the flood, the Tower of Babel.

PUZZLE

Answer these questions. The initial letters of the answers should spell out the name of a person mentioned in the Bible.
1. How many brothers did Abraham have?
2. What river flowed past Ur?
3. What is the name of the Hebrew New Year?
4. Who was the first Hebrew?
5. What city did Abraham's family move to?

CHAPTER II

ABRAHAM IN THE PROMISED LAND

1. TO THE LAND OF CANAAN

ABRAHAM'S FAMILY lived in Haran for several years. One day, as Abraham walked through the fields behind the sheep, he seemed to hear God calling unto him.

"Abraham, Abraham," said God.

"Here I am," replied Abraham.

"Leave your land and your father's home," said God. "Go to the land that I will show you. There you will become the father of a great nation."

Abraham and Sarah got ready to depart.

One of Abraham's favorite nephews, Lot, came to him and said, "I, too, would like to go with you to this new land."

Abraham replied, "Good. Together we will seek this new land. And may our families always dwell together in peace."

Abraham had helped take care of Lot for many years, ever since Lot's father had died in Ur. Abraham, therefore, was very happy that Lot had decided to go with him to seek the promised land.

At last the time came for Abraham to say farewell to his parents and to his brother who remained behind in Haran.

Abraham and Sarah and Lot and their servants traveled slowly on their camels and donkeys. They would pitch their tents near a spring or well where they and their sheep could find water to drink. Sometimes they would remain for many days before they moved on.

They traveled past Damascus until at last they saw the tall mountains of Canaan. And Abraham knew that this was the land that God had promised unto him. Later this land was named the Land of Israel.

Abraham continued his journey until he came to the city of Beth-El. Here he pitched his tent.

One night God appeared to Abraham in a dream. And God said, "This is the land that I shall give unto you and unto your children. I will make a great nation of you. I will bless you; and through you shall all the families of the earth be blessed."

Abraham thanked God for His kindness.

Abraham's arrival in the land of Canaan has been called the beginning of the history of the Hebrew people. This happened 4000 years ago.

2. IN THE NEW LAND

Abraham was received kindly by the people of Canaan. They called him *Ha-Ivri* (The Hebrew). He was called by this name because *Ha-Ivri* means "the one who crossed over." The people knew that Abraham had crossed from the other side of the Euphrates River to come to Canaan.

On the slopes of the hills Abraham found rich pasture land for the flocks. Each winter heavy rains came pouring down to make the soil fertile. Wells and pools provided drinking water. Dates, figs, grapes and other fruits grew in Canaan. From the flocks Abraham could get milk, and from the trees he could obtain honey. That is why Canaan was called "a land flowing with milk and with honey."

Abraham would remain in each place for several months. He would plant seeds, and later gather in the wheat or the barley. When the wells ran dry, Abraham and Lot would fold their tents and move to another place.

From Beth-El they moved south to the Negev. But then came a famine. There was no rain, and the crops were spoiled. There was no food to eat, nor water to drink.

"What shall we do?" asked Lot. "If we stay here we will die, and our flocks will die."

"Let us move south into Egypt," replied Abraham. "We will stay there until the famine is over. Perhaps after the summer the rains will come down once more, and we will be able to return to Canaan."

After a short stay in Egypt, Abraham and Lot returned to Canaan, for again there was food in the land. And they pitched their tents once more near the city of Beth-El.

3. ABRAHAM AND LOT

Abraham became very rich. He had much cattle, and silver and gold.

Lot also had much cattle. Soon the shepherds of Lot began to quarrel with the shepherds of Abraham.

"Get off our land," shouted the servants of Lot.

"This is not your land," replied the shepherds of Abraham. "We too can find pasture for our sheep here."

When Abraham heard of these quarrels he was very sad, for Abraham loved Lot. Abraham wanted to live in peace with his nephew.

Abraham called Lot and said, "Let there be no quarrels between us, for you are my brother's son. And we have always lived together in peace like two brothers."

"Our shepherds quarrel with each other because there is not enough land to support your flocks and my flocks," said Lot.

"Let us part then," said Abraham.

"Where shall I go?" asked Lot.

"Is not the whole land open to us?" said Abraham. "Choose the section of the land that you like best. If you go to the right then I will go to the left. But if you wish to go to the left, then I will go to the right."

Lot looked around and saw the Jordan River beneath the mountains. On both sides of the Jordan was a valley rich in water. This land would be good for the flocks.

"I shall go to the valley of the Jordan," said Lot.

"Then I shall remain in the hill-country," said Abraham.

And Lot took his servants and his sheep to the valley of the Jordan River. And he pitched his tent near the city of Sodom.

And Abraham pitched his tent near the city of Hebron.

4. A HERO IN BATTLE

Now the city of Sodom paid a yearly tax, as tribute, to the king of Elam. For twelve years they paid this tax. In the thirteenth year they sent messengers to four other cities that also paid tribute to the king of Elam.

"Let us rebel against the king of Elam," they said.

"We will fight on your side," replied the other cities.

The king of Sodom and his four allies gathered an army near the Dead Sea. They prepared to fight against the king of Elam.

The king of Elam soon gathered a large army, and fought against Sodom and its allies near the Dead Sea.

The king of Elam easily won the battle. He came into the city of Sodom and captured Lot, and took all the goods that he could find.

The king of Sodom fled in fear. As he ran away he fell into a deep pit from which he could not escape.

That day as Abraham sat in the shade of a large oak tree, he saw a messenger running toward him.

"Help! Help!" shouted the messenger.

"What is wrong?" asked Abraham.

"The city of Sodom has been defeated in battle," said the messenger. "The people of Sodom were all taken prisoner by the king of Elam."

"And what has happened to Lot?" asked Abraham anxiously.

"He too has been captured," replied the messenger.

Fearing for the safety of his nephew, Abraham quickly called unto the young men of Hebron and unto his servants.

"We must march quickly if we hope to rescue our friends," said Abraham.

Three hundred and eighteen men marched with him. They overtook the enemy at night.

"If we attack at night, we will take the enemy by surprise," said Abraham.

That is exactly what happened. The enemy was not prepared to fight back. They did not know that only 318 men marched with Abraham, but thought that a large army was attacking.

In great fright they fled leaving their prisoners and the goods which they had captured.

Abraham rejoiced to find that Lot had not been harmed. He returned after his victory with his men and with the prisoners whom he had freed.

By this time the king of Sodom had been found, and had been raised from the pit by means of a rope. The king then went out to greet Abraham.

"You have won a great victory," said the king. "We owe our lives to you. Give me the people whom you have freed, but the goods you may take for yourself."

"The young men of Hebron who marched with me may take their reward," replied Abraham, "but I will touch nothing. I have sworn unto God that I will not take so much as a thread or a shoe-lace. I do not wish it to be said that the king of Sodom has made me rich."

The king thanked Abraham for his kind deed, and returned to Sodom. Abraham went back with his friends and servants to Hebron.

When the people of the land heard of what Abraham had done they praised him because of his bravery and his kindness.

EXERCISES

I. What is my name? (Review section 1, pages 23 to 24.)
   1. I am the first Hebrew.
   2. I am the mother of the Hebrew people.
   3. I am the city in which Terah and his family lived after they left Ur.
   4. I am the land which God promised unto Abraham and unto his children.
   5. I am the nephew of Abraham. I went with him to find the promised land.

II. Why? (Review sections 2 and 3, pages 24 to 27.)
   1. Why was Abraham called *Ha-Ivri?*
   2. Why is Canaan called a land flowing with milk and with honey?
   3. Why did Abraham go down into Egypt?
   4. Why did Abraham and Lot part from each other?
   5. Why did Lot pick the valley of the Jordan?

III. Fill in the correct name. (Review section 4, pages 27 to 29.)

Abraham, Elam, Hebron, Lot, Sodom

1. The city of Sodom paid tribute to _____.
2. The king of _____ was defeated in battle.
3. _____ was rescued by Abraham.
4. Abraham said, "The young men of _____ may take their reward."
5. The people praised _____ for his bravery and his kindness.

IV. Questions for discussion:
1. Why is it said that Jewish history began when Abraham entered Canaan?
2. Should Abraham have accepted the reward offered by the king of Sodom?
3. We often read about shepherds and their quarrels. Can you tell of any shepherd's quarrel mentioned in the Bible or in any other book?

THINGS TO DO

1. *Television Interviews*—Pretend you are in charge of interviews for a television program. Arrange for interviews with the following people: Abraham, Sarah, Lot, the king of Sodom, the king of Elam. Introduce each person to the class. The members of the class may then address questions to the person being interviewed.

2. *A Map of Abraham's Wanderings*—Consult the maps in the front of the book. Draw a map on which by means of arrows you will show Abraham's wanderings from Ur to Haran, from Haran to Beth-El in Canaan, from Beth-El to the Negev, from the Negev to Egypt and back to Beth-El.

PUZZLE

Fill in the missing 3-letter words. The answers should then spell out the same words whether read *across* or *down*.
1. _____ was Abraham's nephew.
2. Abraham believed in _____ God.
3. "Thou shalt not kill," is one of the _____ commandments.

CHAPTER III

THE DESTRUCTION OF SODOM

1. A WICKED CITY

LOT CONTINUED to live in Sodom for many years. His sheep grazed on the rich pasture-land outside of the city, and Lot became very wealthy.

The people of Sodom, however, were very wicked. They were guilty of many crimes. The judges were unjust and refused to condemn those who were guilty.

The people of Sodom were very cruel to strangers. They would give neither food nor lodging to those who passed through their city.

There is a legend which says that they would offer a special bed to visitors. But if the stranger was too small for the bed, one of the leaders of Sodom would shout, "Stretch him!"

The people would then seize the stranger by his head, his arms and legs and pull until they had stretched his bones so that he could fit into the bed.

If the stranger was too large, the leader would shout, "Crush him!"

The people would then set upon the stranger with clubs

ABRAHAM PRAYING FOR SODOM

and stones, and crush his bones until he was small enough to fit into the bed.

Once a weary stranger came to the city of Sodom. As he entered the gate of the city, he saw several men sitting near the gate of the city.

"Help me," cried the stranger. "I have not eaten for three days. Give me food to eat or I will die."

The men of Sodom laughed when they heard the cry of the stranger.

"This will be good sport to watch," they said to one another. "Let nobody dare to feed him."

Lot's daughter overheard the cry of the stranger. Her heart was moved, and she decided to help him. She called to the stranger and said, "I shall be glad to give you bread to eat. Come with me."

When the people of Sodom found that the stranger had been fed they were very angry.

"Who has dared to disobey us?" they asked.

"Lot's daughter," said somebody.

The people of Sodom were so angry that they decided to punish Lot's daughter. They smeared her body with honey and then exposed her to the bees which stung her many times so that she was in great pain.

God heard the cry of Lot's daughter and said, "The wickedness of Sodom is so great that I shall destroy it."

This story is only a legend, but it does give us some idea of how cruel and wicked the people of Sodom were.

2. ABRAHAM PLEADS FOR SODOM

Near the city of Sodom was a city called Gomorrah. The people of Gomorrah were also very wicked. God decided to destroy both cities.

And God said to Abraham, "The people of Sodom and Gomorrah are very wicked. Their sin is great. Therefore, I shall destroy both cities. Only Lot and his family will I save."

Abraham was very sad when he heard this. Abraham prayed to God to forgive the people.

And Abraham said, "Maybe there are fifty good people in the city. Will you destroy the good people together with the wicked? You are the Judge of all the earth. Surely you will act justly."

And God replied, "If I find fifty good people in Sodom I will forgive all the city for their sake. But there aren't fifty good people."

And Abraham said, "I pray, O Lord, that you will pardon my boldness. Maybe there are just forty-five. Would you not forgive the city for the sake of forty-five good people?"

"Indeed I would," replied God. "But there are not forty-five righteous people in Sodom."

"Maybe there are forty."

"Not even forty."

"Perhaps there are thirty good people."

"No, there are not thirty."

"O Lord, would you not save the city for the sake of twenty righteous persons?" asked Abraham.

"There are not even twenty righteous."

"Please do not be angry with me, O Lord, if I speak but once more. Save the city, I pray you, for the sake of the ten righteous who are found in Sodom."

"Alas, Abraham," said God, "it is a wicked city without even ten righteous people. Only Lot and his family are kind and good. They shall be delivered, but the city I shall destroy with brimstone and with fire."

3. THE TWO MESSENGERS

God sent two messengers to Sodom. They came to Sodom at evening time.

And Lot sat in the gate of Sodom. When he saw the two strangers he rose up to meet them. And Lot greeted them, as was the custom in those days, by bowing down to the ground.

And Lot said, "Behold now, turn aside, I pray you into my house. Rest there during the night. In the morning you may rise up early and go on your way."

The two messengers thanked Lot for his kindness. They knew that Lot had been taught to be kind by Abraham, his uncle. But they refused saying, "We would rather sleep in the open square of the city."

"Do not deny me this favor," urged Lot. "In my house you shall find food and rest. It would please me greatly to be your host."

When the messengers heard Lot's words they replied, "You are very kind. May God reward you for your kindness."

The two men then went with Lot to his home. Here they washed after having walked through the sands of the desert, and prepared to eat. Lot made a feast in honor of his guests and set before them matzot, or unleavened bread.

Just before the men lay down to sleep they heard a great noise. The whole city of Sodom had gathered outside of Lot's house.

"Send out these two men to us," they shouted. "We will show you how to take care of strangers."

Lot feared for the safety of his guests. He went outside and carefully closed the door behind him, so that nobody could enter.

And Lot said, "Please, my friends, do not harm my guests. They have sought protection under my roof, and I will permit nobody to touch them."

"Stand back," they shouted.

But Lot stood in front of the door and barred the way.

"Who are you to tell us what to do?" shouted the people of Sodom. "You yourself are but a stranger, and now you act like a judge. We will treat you worse than we treat your guests."

And they pressed forward seeking to capture Lot.

When the two messengers saw what had happened, they said to Lot, "Fear nothing. God has given us the power to save you."

Quickly they drew Lot within and shut the door. The men of Sodom seized hold of the door and tried to break it down. The messengers of God smote them with blindness so that they searched for the door but could not find it.

At last the people of Sodom grew weary and went away from Lot's house.

4. SODOM IS DESTROYED

As soon as the people of Sodom had left Lot's house the two messengers said to Lot, "We have been sent by the Lord to destroy this city because its sins are so many. But you and your wife and family will be saved. Hurry, gather your daughters and sons-in-law and tell them to leave before it is destroyed."

And Lot believed the messengers. He hurried to the home of his two married daughters and said, "Let us leave Sodom in haste, for God will destroy this city."

The sons-in-law laughed, for they thought that Lot was jesting. Lot sadly returned to his home and told the two angels that only he and his wife and his two unmarried daughters were ready to leave.

In the morning the angels came to Lot and said, "Hurry before it is too late."

Lot lingered for a moment. The men of God took him and his wife and their two daughters by the hand and quickly led them out of the city.

When they stood outside the city one of the angels said, "Escape for your lives! Do not look behind for it is not proper for you to see the destruction of your neighbors."

When Lot and his family had escaped, God began to rain brimstone and fire on Sodom and Gomorrah and on the cities of the plain. And the cities were entirely destroyed.

There is a strange story told about Lot's wife. She was very anxious to see what had happened to the city of Sodom. Disobeying the command of the angel, she turned around to see the destruction of the city. At that instant she turned into a pillar of salt.

The next morning Abraham arose and looked down from the mountain to the plain. And he saw that the cities of the plain had been entirely destroyed. Smoke rose from the land as if from a furnace, and no houses or trace of a city remained.

And Abraham thanked God that He had remembered his nephew Lot and had saved him and his two daughters from the destruction of Sodom.

EXERCISES

I. True or false (Review section 1, pages 32 to 34.)
   1. Lot's sheep grazed in the valley near Sodom.
   2. The judges of Sodom were very fair and just.
   3. There was a very comfortable bed in Sodom for strangers.
   4. Lot's daughter showed kindness to strangers.
   5. The people of Sodom were kind to Lot's daughter.

II. Match: (Review sections 2 and 3, pages 35 to 38.)

Column A	Column B
Gomorrah	1. Prayed for forgiveness to Sodom
Abraham	2. Found lodging in Lot's house
Lot	3. A very wicked city
Messengers	4. Wanted to harm the strangers
Men of Sodom	5. The only kind man in Sodom

III. Who? (Review section 4, pages 38 to 39.)
1. Who was saved from Sodom?
2. Who said, "Escape for your lives"?
3. Who thought Lot was jesting?
4. Who turned into a pillar of salt?
5. Who thanked God for saving his nephew?

IV. Questions for discussion:
1. Compare Abraham and George Washington.
2. Abraham had many good qualities. How many can you list?

THINGS TO DO

1. *An Original Story*—Make up a story for your class newspaper about kindness to a stranger.

2. *Class Mural*—Plan a mural painting based on the life of Abraham as a term project in which all members of the class will take part. Some of the scenes that might be painted are: Abraham breaking the idols; the sailboats of Ur; wandering to Haran; near a well; taking care of the sheep in Canaan; Abraham's tent; Abraham sitting in the shade of the tree; the battle; Abraham praying for Sodom; Lot and his daughters escape from Sodom.

A GAME

Play the game, "What's my name?" One student is picked as leader. A second pupil then tells about a person or a place in the Bible. If the leader guesses the name he remains up, if not the second pupil takes his place. The first pupil who scores five right is the winner.

UNIT TWO

The Children of Abraham

CHAPTER IV

ISHMAEL AND ISAAC

1. THE BIRTH OF ISHMAEL

Now ABRAHAM and Sarah were sad because they had no children.

One night God came to Abraham as he walked in the fields and said, "Abraham, your reward shall be very great."

And Abraham said, "What reward can You give me, since I am childless?"

And God said, "Fear not. You will have children and will become the father of a great nation."

Then God said to Abraham, "Look up at the stars in the heavens."

Abraham raised his eyes and looked up at the stars.

"How many stars do you see?" asked God.

"There are so many that I cannot count them."

"So shall be your seed," said God. "Your descendants shall be as many as the stars of the heavens. And I shall give to them the land of Canaan as an inheritance."

And Abraham told Sarah of God's promise.

Now Sarah had a servant girl named Hagar. In those

days it was the custom for a man to marry more than one wife.

And Sarah said to Abraham, "Since I am childless, take Hagar as your second wife. Perhaps she will bear you children."

And Abraham took Hagar as his second wife.

Hagar became the mother of a boy. And they called the child Ishmael which means, "God has heard."

2. ISAAC

God said to Abraham, "Let there be a covenant, or treaty, between Me and between your descendants. They will carry out My laws of truth and kindness, and I will give unto them the land of Canaan as an inheritance. For each male child that is born this *brith*, or covenant, must be renewed on the eighth day after his birth."

One day as Abraham sat near the door of his tent he saw three men approaching. It was the hottest part of the day and Abraham knew that they must be very tired.

Abraham ran toward the three men and bowed low saying, "If I have found favor in your sight, please do not go away from my tent. Rest here in the shade of a tree. I shall fetch some bread and food. After that you may continue on your journey."

The three men thanked Abraham and sat down to rest.

Abraham hurried to Sarah's tent and said to Sarah, "We have guests who have come to our tent. Make ready three measures of fine meal, and prepare cakes for them."

Then Abraham ran to his servant and told him to prepare a special feast of calf's meat. And the servant did as Abraham had said. Abraham spread out the food under the tree and the strangers ate and drank.

After they had rested one of the strangers said to Abraham, "Where is Sarah, your wife?"

And Abraham replied, "She is in her tent."

And the stranger said, "We have good news. We are messengers from God, and we have come to tell you that next year Sarah will become the mother of a child."

Sarah's tent was nearby, and Sarah heard the words of the messenger. At first Sarah could not believe what she had heard, for she had been childless for so many years.

The messengers then went on their way. These were the same messengers about whom we read in the last chapter, and two of them journeyed to Sodom to save Lot and his family.

Their words came true. A year passed by and Sarah became the mother of a boy. Abraham rejoiced that at last a son was born to him and to Sarah. Abraham called the child's name Isaac which means "laughter," and indeed the child was a source of joy unto all.

3. THE DEPARTURE OF ISHMAEL

People now said, "Abraham is a fitting name, for Abraham means 'father of many nations'; and Sarah too is a fitting name for it means 'princess'." It was at the command of God that Abraham and Sarah were given these names.

Before that their names had been a little different—Abram and Sarai.

Ishmael was thirteen years old when Isaac was born. Abraham became very sad when he saw that Ishmael was not kind to his little brother. As Isaac grew, Ishmael would often shoot his arrows at Isaac. When Abraham scolded him, Ishmael would say that he was jesting.

Sarah was very angry because of this. One day Sarah said to Abraham, "Have you seen how Ishmael treats Isaac?"

"Yes, I have," replied Abraham. "Many times I have told him to be careful and not to practise with his bow and arrow when Isaac is near him."

"It is his mother, Hagar, who is at fault," said Sarah. "She urges Ishmael to tease Isaac. She and her son must be sent away."

"How can I do such a thing?" asked Abraham. "Ishmael is my son. You gave Hagar to me to be my wife. I cannot be so unkind."

"If Hagar remains here there will be serious trouble between Ishmael and Isaac. Ishmael will claim that he deserves to inherit the birthright. It is better to send Ishmael away now."

Abraham did not know what to do. Always he had treated people with kindness. How could he now send Hagar and Ishmael away?

And God said unto Abraham, "Obey the words of Sarah. It is better to send Ishmael away now. Do not fear. I shall protect Ishmael and make of him a great nation, for he too is your child. But Isaac will inherit you."

THE CHILDREN OF ABRAHAM

And Abraham arose in the morning and gave Hagar bread and a pitcher of water. Hagar left with Ishmael for Egypt, but she became lost in the wilderness. Soon there was no water left in the pitcher.

Hagar placed Ishmael in the shade of some shrubs. And Hagar wept for she was afraid that they would die of thirst.

And an angel of God called unto Hagar and said, "Fear not, Hagar, for God has heard your voice. Nearby is a well of water. Lead your son to the well so that he may drink, and God will make of him a great nation."

Hagar looked up and saw the well. She filled the pitcher with water and gave the lad to drink. Afterwards they found the right path.

Hagar and Ishmael lived in the wilderness of Paran. There Abraham visited Ishmael from time to time. Ishmael grew up and became an archer, living by his skill with the bow and arrow.

And Ishmael married an Egyptian girl. Their children continued to live in the desert wandering from place to place. Ishmael became the father of the Arab people.

EXERCISES

I. Who said to whom? (Review section 1, pages 45 to 46.)
  1. "Your reward shall be very great."
  2. "What reward can You give me, since I am childless?"
  3. "You will become the father of a great nation."

4. "Your descendants shall be as many as the stars of the heavens."
5. "Take Hagar as your second wife."

II. Answer each question in a complete sentence. (Review section 2, pages 46 to 47.)
1. What covenant, or treaty, did God make with Abraham?
2. When must this covenant, or *brith*, be renewed?
3. How did Abraham show kindness to the strangers?
4. What news did the messengers bring?
5. What is the meaning of the name "Isaac"?

III. Fill in the correct name—Isaac or Ishmael. (Review section 3, pages 47 to 49.)
1. _____ was the son of Abraham and Sarah.
2. _____ was the older brother.
3. _____ would inherit Abraham.
4. _____ became an archer in the desert.
5. _____ was the father of the Arab nation.

IV. Questions for discussion:
1. What do the Hebrew people and the Arabs have in common?
2. How are the Arabs treated in Israel today?

THINGS TO DO

1. *First Names*—English has borrowed more first names from Hebrew than from any other language. Make a list of famous people or of students who have Biblical first names. Start with the students in your own class. Wherever possible, as in the case of Abraham or Sarah, give the meaning of the name.

2. *Conference on Arabs and Jews*—Pretend that the United Nations has arranged a conference on "How Arabs and Jews Can Work Together." Let each pupil represent a member of the United Nations. Discuss such subjects as trade, peace, education, sports, irrigation and fighting disease.

FINISH THE JINGLE

Hagar was young Ishmael's mother
And little Isaac was his ⎯⎯⎯.

Abraham thanked the Lord who is One
That Sarah, too, had borne a ⎯⎯⎯.

Hagar set out on the path, one day,
But, alas, she lost her ⎯⎯⎯.

Under the shrubs young Ishmael fell
Until his mother found a ⎯⎯⎯.

CHAPTER V

THE STORY OF ISAAC

1. ISAAC GROWS UP

ISAAC'S BOYHOOD was very different from that of a boy today. He learned how to take care of the sheep and how to ride on a camel or on a donkey. He helped his father sow barley or wheat seeds, and learned how to gather in the fruits of an olive or fig tree.

When they decided to move to another place, he would take part in loading their goods on the backs of camels. He would help pitch the tent when they found a new home, and would sometimes help to dig a new well.

Often at night Abraham and his family would gather around the campfire to keep warm. Abraham would tell stories about the days of old, or would teach Isaac about the belief in one God.

Perhaps Isaac asked about the beginning of mankind. And Abraham taught Isaac that although God had made heaven and earth and plants and beasts, He was not satisfied until He made man in His own image.

"All men are brothers," said Abraham, "for Adam was the father of all men."

THE CHILDREN OF ABRAHAM

AROUND THE CAMPFIRE

Abraham taught Isaac that God wanted man to be good. He told his son that God was angry when Cain killed his brother, and when the people in Noah's time did wrong. Abraham also told Isaac the story of the flood which he had heard when he was a boy in Ur.

"God has made a covenant with us," said Abraham. "We and our descendants must carry out God's law of truth and of kindness, and God will give unto our children the land of Canaan. You must always live up to this covenant."

And Isaac promised that he would try to be true to this covenant.

2. THE SACRIFICE OF THE RAM

Abraham now had to meet his hardest test. God decided to try Abraham to see whether he was really faithful.

One day God said, "Abraham, Abraham."

And Abraham replied, "Here I am."

And God said, "Take your beloved son, Isaac, and bring him up as a sacrifice unto Me."

Abraham did not know what to do. He loved his son dearly, but how could he disobey the word of God?

The next day Abraham called unto Isaac and unto two of his servants. They traveled for two days until they came to Mount Moriah.

And Abraham said unto the two servants, "Stay here with the donkey, and Isaac and I will worship God on the mountain top."

Abraham took the wood for the sacrifice, and he and Isaac walked together toward the mountain.

And Isaac said, "My father."

"What is it, my son?" asked Abraham.

"I see the wood for the fire, but where is the lamb for the sacrifice?"

"God will provide a lamb," replied Abraham.

At last they came to the top of Mount Moriah. Abraham built an altar, laid the wood in place and then bound Isaac to the altar.

With tears in his eyes Abraham got ready to sacrifice his son.

Just then a voice called from heaven, "Abraham, Abraham."

And Abraham said, "Here am I."

And the angel of God said, "Do not lay your hand on Isaac. Now I know how faithful you are, for you did not disobey the word of God."

Abraham looked up and saw a ram caught by its horns in a tree. Abraham took the ram and sacrificed it on the altar in place of Isaac.

And the angel of God called again and said, "Because you have obeyed the voice of God, you and your children will be blessed; and all the nations of the world will be blessed through you."

Abraham returned with Isaac unto the two servants and rejoiced that no harm had come to his son.

The ram's horn or *shofar* is sounded in the synagogue each Rosh Ha-Shanah or New Year's Day. The sound of the *shofar* is a call to freedom; it also warns the people to rid themselves of their sins. But it reminds us, too, of the sacrifice of the ram, which was caught by its horns in the tree, in place of Isaac. That is why on each Rosh Ha-Shanah day we read again this story of how Abraham obeyed the voice of God.

3. THE DEATH OF SARAH

Sarah was happy to see her son grow into manhood as a wise, good and kind young man. She knew that he would carry out the covenant which God had made with Abraham, and that he would teach many people to believe in one God.

Sarah reached a ripe old age and then died in the city of **Hebron**. Many came to mourn the passing of this great woman, the mother of the Hebrew nation. Abraham and Isaac were very sad.

And Abraham said, "I must provide a proper burial-place for this great woman."

Abraham came to Ephron who lived in Hebron and said, "Sell me the field of Machpelah which belongs to you. I shall pay you whatever the field is worth, for this field will be a fitting burial-place for Sarah."

And Ephron replied, "Hear me, O Abraham. The field is yours. I give it to you. My friends and neighbors are witness that you may take the field as a burial-place for Sarah."

And Abraham bowed down and said, "Hear me, O Ephron. I thank you for letting me have the field. But I do not want it as a present. Tell me how much the field is worth and I shall give you the silver."

And Ephron replied, "What are 400 shekels between friends? Take the field, for it is yours."

Abraham took 400 pieces of silver and gave it unto Ephron who gladly took the money even though he had offered the field as a gift.

Abraham then buried Sarah in the field of Machpelah. Later the other Hebrew forefathers were also buried here.

To this very day travelers from all over the world visit Hebron to honor the founders of the Hebrew people.

EXERCISES

I. What were some of Isaac's boyhood activities? List at least four. (Review section 1, pages 53 to 54.)

II. True or false? (Review section 2, pages 54 to 56.)
1. Abraham disobeyed the word of God.
2. Isaac asked, "Where is the lamb for the sacrifice?"
3. Abraham built the altar on Mount Hebron.
4. Abraham sacrificed a ram in place of Isaac.
5. We read this story in the synagogue on Rosh Ha-Shanah.

III. Fill in the correct name. (Review section 3, pages 56 to 57.)

ABRAHAM, EPHRON, ISAAC, MACHPELAH, SARAH
1. _____ mourned for his mother.
2. _____ offered the field as a gift.
3. _____ paid 400 shekels for the field.
4. The field of _____ is in Hebron.
5. _____ is the mother of the Hebrew people.

IV. Subjects for discussion:
1. Compare the activities of a boy in Isaac's time with the activities of a boy today.
2. The story of the sacrifice of the ram in place of Isaac is read in the synagogue on Rosh Ha-Shanah. Mention other Rosh Ha-Shanah customs.

THINGS TO DO

1. *Shofar*—Draw a picture of a man blowing a shofar on Rosh Ha-Shanah. Add greetings for the New Year.
2. *Make-Believe Campfire*—Arrange a make-believe campfire like the campfires attended by Abraham and Isaac. Each pupil can tell his favorite holiday story or Bible story, or sing his favorite Hebrew song.

CONTEST

Divide the class into two teams. Each pupil is asked a question based on one of the stories in this book. The team that answers the most questions correctly is the winner.

CHAPTER VI

THE BEAUTIFUL REBECCA

1. ELIEZER'S MISSION

ABRAHAM was proud of his son Isaac who had now grown to manhood. Abraham was afraid that Isaac might marry one of the daughters of the Canaanites.

"Such a wife might lead him astray," thought Abraham. "The Canaanites worship idols. A Canaanite wife might teach Isaac's children to bow down to idols. She will make her husband forget our covenant with God to carry out the laws of kindness and of mercy."

Abraham hoped that Isaac would find a wife from among the members of his family who had remained in Haran.

Abraham then spoke unto his chief servant, Eliezer. "Go to the land from which I came, to my relatives, to find a wife for my son, Isaac. Swear that you will not pick a wife from among the Canaanites."

"How do I know that I will find the right girl for Isaac?" asked Eliezer.

"God will direct your steps so that your mission will be successful," said Abraham.

"Perhaps the girl will not want to leave her country. What shall I do then? Shall I bring back Isaac to the land from which you have come?"

"If the woman refuses to return, you are free of any guilt. But beware not to bring Isaac back to the land from which I came."

It was the custom then to swear by placing one's hand on the other person's thigh. So Eliezer put his hand on Abraham's thigh, and he swore that he would look for a wife among Abraham's relatives.

And Abraham gave Eliezer 10 camels. On these camels were placed gold and silver and supplies. Several men went with Eliezer to Haran.

Eliezer began to travel slowly toward the river of Euphrates, to the city in which Abraham's family lived. At last after many days he arrived at the city of Haran in the Land of the Two Rivers.

Outside of the city was a large well of water, and here Eliezer made his camels kneel down to rest.

2. REBECCA AT THE WELL

It was almost evening when Eliezer rested near the well. Just at this time of the day the young girls would go out to draw water from the well.

And Eliezer prayed unto God, "O Lord, God of my master Abraham, send me, I pray You, good speed this day, and show kindness unto my master Abraham."

And Eliezer thought to himself, "Let this be the sign that I have found the right girl. I shall ask each maiden to draw water in her pitcher for me. If the girl offers to draw water for my camels too, then I will know that she is kind and good. This is the girl whom God has chosen for Isaac."

At this moment a beautiful girl named Rebecca came to the well. Eliezer noticed that the girl was very fair to look upon. He watched as she went down to the fountain and filled her pitcher with water.

Eliezer ran to meet her saying, "Please give me a little water to drink. I am very thirsty after my long journey."

And Rebecca said, "Drink, my lord."

Rebecca lowered her pitcher from her shoulder, and gave Eliezer water to drink. When he had satisfied his thirst, Rebecca said, "I shall draw water again for your camels so that they too might drink."

She hurried to the fountain and drew water for the ten camels. Whenever the pitcher was empty she would return to the well, and fill it again.

Eliezer wondered, "Is this the maiden whom God has picked for my master's son?"

When she had finished drawing water for the camels, Eliezer asked, "What is your name, my dear maiden?"

"Rebecca," she replied.

"Whose daughter are you?"

"I am the daughter of Bethuel."

Eliezer rejoiced to hear this answer, for Bethuel was Abraham's nephew.

"I have come from the home of Abraham, your father's

uncle," said Eliezer. "Is there place in your father's house for me to lodge this night?"

"You are most welcome," said Rebecca. "Indeed there is room for you. My father will be very happy to see you and to receive greetings from Abraham."

Eliezer opened the sack on one of the camels, and took out a golden ring and two golden bracelets.

"Here is a gift from my master," said Eliezer.

Rebecca thanked the servant for his kindness and then ran to tell her father about their guest.

3. A WIFE FOR ISAAC

Bethuel was greatly pleased to hear of the arrival of Eliezer. He turned to his son, Laban, saying, "Laban, go out to welcome Eliezer."

Laban quickly ran to the fountain.

"Welcome," he said to Eliezer. "Come in; why do you stand outside? I have made room for you, for the men who are with you and for your camels."

Eliezer went with Laban. Then they set food before him.

"I shall not eat until I have spoken of my mission," said Eliezer.

"Speak," said Bethuel and Laban.

Eliezer told them his story. He told them how Abraham had sent him to find a wife for Isaac. He also told them how Rebecca had proved that she was the right person for Isaac.

REBECCA AND ISAAC

"And now," said Eliezer, "if you will deal kindly with my master, tell me. And if not, tell me so that I shall know what to do."

"This all comes from God," replied Bethuel. "Let Rebecca be Isaac's wife as the Lord has spoken."

Eliezer gave thanks to God that he had been successful in his mission. He brought out jewels of silver and of gold and garments, and gave them as presents to Rebecca and her brother and her parents.

Eliezer rose early in the morning and said, "Now let me return unto my master."

"Let Rebecca remain with us a few days," said Laban. "After that she may go."

"Please do not delay my return journey," replied Eliezer.

"We will call Rebecca and ask her what she wishes to do," said her mother.

They called Rebecca and told her how anxious Eliezer was to leave immediately.

"Will you go right away or do you want to wait?" they asked.

"I will go as soon as Eliezer wishes to leave," replied Rebecca.

Her parents and brother blessed her, and she said farewell. After many days' journey they arrived in Canaan.

That day Isaac went out to walk in the fields. In the distance he saw camels approaching. With great joy he discovered it was Eliezer who had succeeded in his mission.

Isaac loved Rebecca dearly and soon married her. Abraham rejoiced that Eliezer had found such a good wife for Isaac.

EXERCISES

I. Complete each sentence by choosing the correct word or phrase. (Review section 1, pages 59 to 60.)
1. Abraham did not want Isaac to marry a Canaanite girl because the Canaanites (*a*—were poor, *b*—were his enemies, *c*—worshiped idols).
2. Abraham's servant was named (*a*—Eliezer, *b*—Ephron, *c*—Laban).
3. Abraham said it would not be Eliezer's fault (*a*—if he found a Canaanite girl for Isaac, *b*—if he made Isaac return to the land from which Abraham had come, *c*—if the girl did not want to leave her country to go to Canaan).
4. Eliezer rode on (*a*—camels, *b*—donkeys, *c*—horses).

II. Answer each question in a complete sentence. (Review section 2, pages 60 to 62.)
1. When would the girls come out to draw water?
2. How would Eliezer know whom God had chosen to be Isaac's wife?
3. Who came to draw water?
4. How did Rebecca prove that she was kind?
5. What gift did Eliezer give to Rebecca?

III. Who said to whom? (Review section 3, pages 62 to 64.)
1. "Come in; why do you stand outside?"
2. "I shall not eat until I have spoken of my mission."
3. "Let Rebecca be Isaac's wife as the Lord has spoken."
4. "Please do not delay my return journey."
5. "I will go as soon as Eliezer wishes to leave."

IV. Questions for discussion:
1. Why didn't Abraham want Isaac to return to the country from which he had come?
2. What are some interesting customs mentioned in this chapter?

REVIEW QUESTIONS

for Units One and Two (pages 15 to 66)

1. In your opinion which was the most important event in Abraham's life?
2. Which story is your favorite? Why?
3. Identify: Ur, Terah, Haran, Euphrates, Canaan, Lot, Jordan, Gomorrah, Sodom, Ishmael, Hagar, Eliezer, Laban, Bethuel.

TEST

on Units One and Two

I. True or false? (30 points)

1. Abraham, instead of believing in idols, believed in one God.
2. Abraham was born in Haran.
3. God promised Canaan to Abraham and to his descendants.
4. After the quarrel with Lot, Abraham settled in the valley of the Jordan.
5. Abraham became rich when he defeated Elam.
6. The people of Sodom were kind to strangers.
7. Ishmael was Isaac's older brother.
8. Isaac was the father of the Arab people.
9. The ram was sacrificed instead of Isaac.
10. Abraham did not want Isaac to marry a Canaanite girl.

THE CHILDREN OF ABRAHAM

II. Match: (20 points)

Column A	Column B
Euphrates	1. Sarah's burial-place
Machpelah	2. The promised land
Sodom	3. A river that flowed past Ur
Haran	4. A wicked city
Canaan	5. The city in which Abraham's family settled

III. Why? (30 points)
1. Why is Abraham called the first Hebrew?
2. Why did Abraham leave Haran?
3. Why did Abraham and Lot separate?
4. Why did Abraham send Hagar away?
5. Why did Eliezer pick Rebecca as Isaac's wife?

IV. Complete: (20 points)
1. Many boats came to the city of _____. (Ur, Hebron)
2. Lot was taken captive by the king of _____. (Elam, Sodom)
3. The mother of Ishmael was _____. (Sarah, Hagar)
4. Isaac means _____. ("laughter", "father of many nations")
5. The brother of Rebecca was named _____. (Laban, Bethuel)

UNIT THREE

Jacob

CHAPTER VII

JACOB AND ESAU

1. ISAAC—SUCCESSOR TO ABRAHAM

ABRAHAM, who was now very old, thanked God for all the blessings he had received. He rejoiced when two sons, Esau and Jacob, were born to Rebecca and Isaac. Abraham remembered God's promise to make a mighty nation of his descendants, and he was happy.

When Abraham died he was buried next to Sarah in the field of Machpelah. Many people in Canaan mourned the passing of this great man.

There are many reasons why Abraham may be called one of the greatest leaders we have ever had.

1. He was the father of the Hebrew people.
2. He was the first to teach the belief in one God. Today most people have accepted the belief in one God. The Jewish religion is really the mother of most modern religions.
3. He made Canaan the homeland of the Hebrew people by obeying God's command to go to the promised land.
4. He taught that God wants kindness and justice.

5. He accepted a covenant between God and the Hebrew people. If the people obeyed God's law, Canaan would be given to them as an inheritance.

6. He was a hero in battle, and protected his neighbors.

7. He was a man of peace who helped cultivate the land and who treated all men kindly.

Isaac proved to be a worthy successor to Abraham. He, too, was a man of peace. He took care of his sheep, and sowed seeds in the earth, gathering in each season the rich crops.

God appeared unto Isaac and said, "I will be with you and I will bless you. And I will keep the promise I made unto Abraham to give you this land, and to make your descendants like the stars of heaven."

The Philistines who lived in the Negev, or south, soon began to cause trouble. After Abraham's death, they filled all the wells he had dug with earth.

Isaac who was a man of peace did not want to quarrel with the Philistines over the wells.

"Let us dig another well," he said to his servants.

They dug another well, but the Philistine shepherds said, "This is our water."

Isaac moved his flocks and dug another well, but again the Philistines said, "This well belongs to us."

When the king of the Philistines saw that God had blessed Isaac, he decided to make peace with him. He came to Beer-sheba where Isaac had pitched his tent, and said, "Let there be peace between us."

Isaac prepared a feast for the king in honor of the treaty

of peace. As they sat at the feast, Isaac's servants ran in and said, "We have found water! We have found water!"

"There is enough water in this land for you and for me," said Isaac to the Philistines. "We do not have to quarrel, for the land can support both of us."

After that Isaac and his neighbors lived in peace, and God blessed Isaac as He had promised.

2. THE BIRTHRIGHT

Isaac and Rebecca had two sons, Esau and Jacob. They were twins, but Esau was born a few minutes before Jacob.

The custom was that the oldest child became head of the tribe or family after his father's death. This was called the birthright.

Since Esau was a few minutes older than Jacob the birthright belonged to him. But Esau cared very little about the birthright or about being leader. Esau was a cunning hunter, and all he cared about was hunting game.

Jacob was a quiet man who remained in his tent. Jacob often thought about God, and about the covenant between God and the Hebrew people.

Rebecca noticed the difference between Jacob and Esau.

"Esau does not deserve the birthright," said Rebecca to Isaac. "He is a wild hunter and will not make a good leader. Jacob will make a better leader, one who will rule with kindness and with justice."

Isaac did not answer. He loved to eat of the game caught by Esau, and he did not see why Esau would not be a good leader. Rebecca would often tell Jacob that he really deserved the birthright.

One day Esau went hunting in the fields, but he caught nothing. When he returned he was faint with hunger.

That day Jacob had prepared a pottage or stew. When Esau saw the pottage he said in a rough voice, "Let me swallow some of this red, red pottage for I am faint with hunger."

Jacob remembered what Rebecca often told him about the birthright, and thought that this would be a good chance to settle the question of the birthright.

"You may have as much of the pottage as you wish," said Jacob, "but first sell me your birthright."

"What good will the birthright do me? Here I am dying of hunger," said Esau. "You can have the birthright."

Esau was not dying at all, although he was quite hungry. He just did not care about the birthright.

"Swear," said Jacob.

"Of course I swear," said Esau. "Who cares about the birthright? Just let me have something to eat."

Esau's words showed how little he deserved the birthright. But even though Jacob deserved the birthright more than Esau, he was later punished by God for obtaining the birthright through cunning.

3. THE BLESSING

Isaac became blind in his old age.

One day he called Esau, and said, "My son."

"Here am I," replied Esau.

"I am old," said Isaac, "and do not know how soon I shall die. Take your bow and arrow and hunt game. And make me tasty food such as I love. Bring it to me and I shall eat, and I shall bless you before I die."

Esau went out to the fields to hunt game as his father had told him.

Rebecca heard when Isaac spoke to her son.

"Esau does not deserve a special blessing," thought Rebecca. "It is Jacob who should receive this blessing."

Rebecca spoke to Jacob, saying, "I heard your father ask Esau to hunt game and to bring him tasty food so that he might bless him. Now do as I say. Bring two kids from the flock. I shall make food such as your father loves and he will bless you before he dies."

Jacob did not want to deceive his father.

"Esau is a hairy man," he said, "and I am smooth. Isaac will feel me and find out that I am Jacob. He will curse me instead of blessing me."

"I am your mother and you must do as I say," replied Rebecca. "If your father finds out what we have done, the blame will fall upon me. But I know that I am doing the right thing."

Jacob was sad at the thought of deceiving Isaac, but he knew that he must obey Rebecca. He fetched two kids from the flock, and Rebecca prepared tasty food. The skins of the kids she placed on Jacob's hands and neck so that he would seem hairy like Esau.

Jacob came to Isaac and said, "My father."

"Here am I," said Isaac. "Who are you, my son?"

"I am Esau," said Jacob. "Arise and eat of the food I have prepared so that your soul may bless me."

"How is it that you have come back so soon?" asked Isaac.

"I had good luck and found game immediately," said Jacob.

"Come near that I may feel you," said Isaac, "to see whether you are really Esau."

Isaac felt Jacob's hands which were covered with the goat's hair, and thought it was really Esau.

And Isaac said, "The voice is the voice of Jacob, but the hands are the hands of Esau."

Isaac ate the food, and Jacob brought him wine and he drank.

Isaac said, "Come near now, and kiss me my son."

Jacob came near and kissed Isaac.

Isaac blessed Jacob saying,

> "May God give you of the dew of heaven,
> And of the fat places of the earth,
> And plenty of corn and wine.
> Let peoples serve you,
> And nations bow down to you."

Jacob thanked Isaac and left. As soon as Jacob had left, Esau came back from his hunting. He prepared food and came to Isaac saying, "Arise my father and eat of the food that I have prepared."

And Isaac trembled. "Who then just came with food and obtained my blessing?"

JACOB

When Esau heard the words of his father, he cried out, "Bless me too, O my father."

Isaac said, "It must have been your brother, Jacob. I have blessed him, and he shall remain blessed."

And Esau said, "First he took my birthright and now my blessing. Do you not have a blessing for me?"

Isaac answered, "I have already given him and his descendants the greater blessing. But you too shall be blessed. You will live by your sword, and you will dwell in a fertile land that is watered by the dew of heaven."

Then Esau hated Jacob. And Esau said, "After my father's death I will kill Jacob."

EXERCISES

I. Answer each question in a complete sentence. (Review section 1, pages 71 to 73.)
  1. Why is Abraham one of our greatest leaders? (Mention 2 reasons.)
  2. What promise did God make to Isaac?
  3. What did the Philistines do after the death of Abraham?
  4. How did Isaac prove that he loved peace?
  5. Where did Isaac pitch his tent?

II. Jacob or Esau? (Review section 2, pages 73 to 74.)
  1. _____ was the older brother.
  2. Rebecca thought that _____ deserved the birthright.
  3. _____ was a quiet man who remained in his tent.

4. _____ said, "Let me swallow some of this red, red pottage."
5. _____ sold his birthright for some pottage.

III. Complete: (Review section 3, pages 74 to 77.)

        Rebecca, Isaac, Esau, Jacob

1. _____ became blind.
2. _____ wanted Jacob to receive the blessing.
3. _____ was given the greater blessing.
4. _____ was told that he would live by his sword.

IV. Questions for discussion:
1. In what ways was Isaac like Abraham?
2. Why is it important for us to study about the heroes of our people?

THINGS TO DO

1. *A Play*—Act out the story of Jacob and Esau in two scenes: Scene 1—The Birthright; Scene 2—The Blessing.
2. *Bible Dictionary*—Arrange a dictionary of the people and places mentioned in the Bible. Under each letter list the name, and something important about the person or place. You might include a brief design on each page.

A HISTORY GAME

One pupil goes out of the room. The other pupils choose the name of a person or place. The student who is "it" then asks 5 questions. The answers must be either "yes" or "no". The student must guess what name the class has picked.

CHAPTER VIII

JACOB IN HARAN

1. JACOB'S DREAM

REBECCA was told that Esau planned to kill Jacob. "Jacob must leave Canaan and go to Haran," thought Rebecca, "until Esau's anger passes."

Now Esau had married a Canaanite girl, and his parents were greatly displeased. Rebecca came to Isaac, and said, "I am weary of my life because of Esau's marriage. If Jacob marries a Canaanite girl, what good shall my life be to me?"

Isaac then called Jacob and said, "Arise, go to Haran, to the Land of the Two Rivers, to your mother's house. There you will find a wife from your mother's family. May God bless you with the blessing he gave to Abraham, and may you inherit this land which God has promised unto Abraham and unto his descendants."

Jacob kissed Rebecca and Isaac and then set out on foot for Haran. He left Beer-sheba and traveled until he came to Beth-El.

The sun set, and Jacob thought, "I shall lodge here for the night."

He picked a large stone and placed it under his head as a pillow, and lay down on the ground and slept.

Soon Jacob began to dream. He dreamed that he saw a ladder that reached from the earth to the sky. And he dreamed that he saw angels on the ladder. Some climbed down from heaven to earth and other angels climbed up from earth to heaven.

Just then he dreamed that he heard the voice of God. And God said, "I am the Lord, the God of Abraham and the God of Isaac. The land on which you now lie, I will give to you and to your children. I will be with you wherever you go, and I will bring you back to this land. Your descendants shall be a blessing unto the entire world."

And Jacob awoke out of his sleep and said, "Surely this is a holy place. This is none other than the house of God, and this is the gate of heaven."

From then on the place was called "Beth-El" (the house of God).

Jacob took the stone on which he had slept, and set it up as a monument to God. And Jacob prayed that God be with him so that he might return in peace to the house of his father.

2. AT THE WELL

Jacob continued on his journey until he arrived in the Land of the Two Rivers.

He came to a well in the field. On the mouth of the

well was a large stone. Nearby were flocks of sheep lying in the field.

Jacob turned to the shepherds and asked, "What city do you come from?"

"We are from the city of Haran," they replied.

"Do you know Laban?" asked Jacob.

"Yes, we know him," they said.

"Is it well with him?"

"It is well with him," answered the shepherds.

"Look," said one of the shepherds. "His daughter Rachel is coming with the sheep."

While they were waiting for Rachel to come near, Jacob said to the shepherds, "Why do you not water the sheep? The day is yet long. You must feed the sheep before you gather them together for the evening."

"We cannot," replied the shepherds, "because the stone is too large. When all the shepherds are gathered together then we shall roll away the stone and water our flocks."

When Rachel came near, Jacob ran to her and said, "I am Jacob, the son of Isaac and Rebecca."

"Welcome to Haran," said Rachel. "My father will rejoice to see you."

And Jacob kissed Rachel, his cousin; tears of joy welled up in his eyes that at last he had completed his journey.

"Let me help you roll away the stone, and water your flocks," said Jacob.

He ran to the stone and without the help of any of the shepherds rolled away the large stone. The shepherds wondered at his great strength.

Jacob quickly watered Rachel's flock. Rachel, meanwhile, ran to her home to tell her father, Laban, the glad news.

When Laban heard of Jacob's arrival, he came out to meet him. He embraced him and kissed him.

"Welcome, most welcome, my dear nephew," said Laban.

Laban brought Jacob to his home. He prepared a feast in his honor and asked about the welfare of his sister, Rebecca, and about Isaac.

"Let this be as your own home," said Laban to Jacob, "for you are my own flesh and blood."

Jacob thanked Laban for his kindness, and remained in Laban's home serving as one of his shepherds. He soon fell deeply in love with the beautiful Rachel.

3. RACHEL AND LEAH

Jacob served as a shepherd for about a month. Because of his great strength he was able to roll away the stone from the mouth of the well each day by himself. Laban saw that he was an excellent shepherd.

Laban then came to Jacob and said, "You have served me these past four weeks without reward. Even though you are my nephew it is not fair for me to withhold your wages. Tell me, what shall be your wages for your work?"

Jacob immediately answered, "I shall serve you for seven years without pay, if I can marry Rachel at the end of the seven years."

JACOB THE SHEPHERD

Now Laban had an older daughter named Leah. Laban was not too happy when he heard Jacob's reply for he had hoped that Jacob would marry Leah, his older daughter.

Laban did not mention this to Jacob. Instead he said, "Let it be as you say. Surely it is better for Rachel to marry one of my own family than to marry a stranger."

But Laban thought to himself, "It shall not be as Jacob thinks."

For seven years Jacob served Laban. He worked hard in the fields, but the years passed quickly so great was Jacob's love for Rachel.

At last the seven years were ended.

Jacob came to Laban and said, "The time has come for me to marry Rachel."

Laban invited many of his friends and neighbors to the wedding feast. It was the custom for the bride to wear a heavy veil so that her face was entirely covered.

After the wedding Jacob lifted the veil of the bride, and discovered to his surprise that he had been married to Leah instead of to Rachel.

In great anger Jacob came to Laban and said, "Why have you deceived me? Did I not serve you for Rachel?"

And Laban said, "It is the custom in our country for the older daughter to marry first. It would have been wrong for Rachel to marry before Leah."

"But it is Rachel that I love," said Jacob.

"Do not be angry," replied Laban. "You may marry Rachel too. At the end of the seven days of celebration in honor of Leah, you may marry Rachel. Then you can serve me another seven years in return for my younger daughter."

Since it was the custom then for a man to marry more than one wife, Jacob agreed to what Laban had said. He married Rachel and served Laban another seven years.

And Jacob was blessed by God with many children.

EXERCISES

I. Complete: (Review section 1, pages 79 to 80.)
  1. _____ heard about Esau's plan. (Rebecca, Jacob)
  2. _____ told Jacob to go to Haran. (Rebecca, Isaac)
  3. Esau married a girl from _____. (Egypt, Canaan)
  4. Jacob began his journey from _____. (Haran, Beer-sheba)
  5. Beth-El means _____. (the gate of heaven, the house of God)

II. Who? (Review section 2, pages 80 to 82.)
  1. Who said, "We are from Haran"?
  2. Who met Jacob at the well?
  3. Who rolled away the stone without the help of others?
  4. Who was Laban's sister?
  5. Who invited Jacob to remain in his home?

III. Rachel or Leah? (Review section 3, pages 82 to 85.)
  1. Laban's older daughter was named _____.
  2. Jacob loved _____.
  3. Laban promised that _____ would become Jacob's wife.

4. Jacob was surprised when he found out that _____ was his bride.
5. Jacob worked another seven years for _____.

IV. Questions for discussion:
1. Why were Esau's parents displeased when he married a Canaanite girl?
2. God promised that the Hebrew people would be a blessing unto the entire world. Mention some ways in which the Hebrew people have enriched mankind.

THINGS TO DO

1. *Class Exhibit*—Make an exhibit or diorama of shepherd life. Include the tents, the shepherds and their flocks, the well, a camel caravan.

2. *Shepherd Life*—Bring in a report to class about shepherd life.

PUZZLE

Which person or place mentioned in this book has only 2 letters in its name? 3 letters? 4 letters? 5 letters? 6 letters? 7 letters? 8 letters? 9 letters?

CHAPTER IX

JACOB'S RETURN TO CANAAN

1. JACOB FLEES FROM LABAN

AFTER JACOB had served Laban for fourteen years, he was anxious to return to Isaac and Rebecca.

Jacob came to Laban and said, "I have served you for fourteen years. Now I wish to return to my own country and to the house of my parents."

Laban replied, "Do not leave me, for God has blessed me because of you. Tell me what wages you wish and I shall pay you for your work."

Jacob told Laban what wages he would expect in return for his service. Laban agreed, but later tried to cheat Jacob. God, however, was with Jacob, and Jacob prospered. He became the owner of sheep and goats and cattle.

When Laban and his sons saw how rich Jacob had become, they were very jealous.

"Jacob has become rich at the expense of our father," said Laban's sons.

Jacob saw that Laban and his family were not friendly any longer. One night God appeared to Jacob in a dream and said, "Return unto the land of your fathers, and I will be with you."

Jacob had now served Laban for twenty years and he knew that the time had come for him to return.

He called Rachel and Leah unto him and said, "Your father, Laban, is no longer friendly toward me. I have served him faithfully for twenty years. He has cheated me many times, but God has blessed me and I have become wealthy. Let us go back to Canaan to the house of my father and mother."

Rachel and Leah replied, "We are like strangers in our father's house. We will do as you say."

Jacob was afraid to tell Laban of his plans for he knew that Laban would not allow him to depart. He waited until Laban had gone away to shear his sheep.

Then Jacob arose and set his family on camels, and fled from Laban.

2. LABAN PURSUES JACOB

Jacob crossed the Euphrates River and journeyed toward Canaan.

Three days passed by before Laban found out that Jacob and his family had fled from Haran. Laban was very angry when he heard the news, and he and his sons began to pursue after Jacob.

After seven days Jacob reached Mount Gilead. It was there that Laban overtook him. But God appeared to Laban in a dream and said, "Beware not to harm Jacob in any way."

When Laban saw Jacob he said angrily, "Why did you run away from me? And why did you carry away my daughters as if they were captives?"

"I was afraid you would try to take Rachel and Leah from me by force," said Jacob.

"You have done foolishly," said Laban, "for I did not even have a chance to say farewell and to kiss my children and grandchildren. I would have made a great feast in your honor and would have sent you away with music and with singing."

Laban then searched through Jacob's tents to see what he had taken with him.

"Why have you pursued after me?" said Jacob in anger to Laban. "Why do you search my goods? Have I wronged you in any way? For twenty years I served you faithfully and allowed no harm to befall a single lamb. During the day I was consumed by the sun, and at night by the frost. Yet I guarded your flocks so that all would be well with them."

Laban was a little ashamed that he had not treated Jacob more kindly.

"Let us not quarrel," he said. "After all, Leah and Rachel are my own daughters. God, too, has warned me not to harm you in any way. Let us make a treaty of friendship with each other."

Jacob took a large stone which he set up as a sign of their treaty. Both Laban and Jacob swore that they would not pass beyond this stone to harm the other.

Laban and Jacob broke bread together and feasted that night.

The next morning Laban arose; he kissed his daughters and grandchildren and blessed them. And Laban returned to Haran and Jacob continued on his journey to Canaan.

3. REUNION WITH ESAU

Jacob was worried about his brother's actions.

"What will Esau do?" he asked himself. "Will he seek revenge or will he welcome me back to Canaan?"

Jacob sent messengers to Esau.

"Say unto Esau that I have returned and that I have a rich present for him."

The messengers soon came back to Jacob with these words: "We gave Esau your message, and he is coming to meet you with 400 men."

Jacob now feared for the safety of his family for Esau and his 400 men could easily destroy them all.

Jacob quickly divided his family into two camps.

"If Esau attacks one camp at least the other will escape," thought Jacob.

Early the next morning Jacob called one of his servants and gave him a herd of camels.

"Go before me," said Jacob to the servant.

"When Esau asks who you are and to whom the camels belong, say that they are a present to him from Jacob."

Jacob gave a second servant a herd of goats, and told him to deliver the same message to Esau. The third servant was given donkeys, a fourth servant was given cows. Each servant was told to present the animals to Esau as a gift.

Later a messenger came running to Jacob and said, "Your brother, Esau, is coming."

Jacob looked up and recognized his brother who was escorted by 400 men. What did Esau intend to do? Jacob prayed to God that all would be well.

He bowed low and then came near to his brother. Esau ran forward to meet him. He embraced Jacob and kissed him.

"Welcome, my brother, welcome," said Esau.

Both rejoiced that after so many years they were reunited in peace.

Esau pointed to Rachel and Leah and the children and asked, "Who are these?"

"This is the family with which God has blessed me," replied Jacob as he introduced each one to Esau.

"And what is the meaning of all this?" asked Esau pointing to the camels and goats and donkeys and cattle which Jacob had sent to him.

"Accept it as a gift," said Jacob.

And Esau said, "I have enough, my brother. Keep what is yours."

And Jacob replied, "If I have found favor in your eyes, please accept this present. God has been very generous with me, and I am happy to share my wealth with my brother."

Esau accepted the present, thanking Jacob for his kindness.

Esau then went back to his home in Edom while Jacob crossed the Jordan River and returned to Canaan.

Isaac and Rebecca rejoiced to see Jacob and his family. They were very happy that the quarrel had been forgotten, and that Esau no longer planned to harm Jacob.

Jacob and Esau lived in peace for the rest of their lives. When Isaac and Rebecca died at a ripe old age, the two brothers buried them in the field of Machpelah, next to Abraham and Sarah.

Jacob was now given another name—Israel, which means "Champion of God." From then on his children were called Israelites or Hebrews.

EXERCISES

I. Why? (Review section 1, pages 87 to 88.)
1. Why did Laban ask Jacob to continue to work for him?
2. Why were Laban's sons jealous of Jacob?
3. Why did Jacob decide to return after 20 years?
4. Why did Rachel and Leah agree to leave their father's house?
5. Why didn't Jacob tell Laban of his plan to leave?

II. True or false? (Review section 2, pages 88 to 90.)
1. Seven days passed before Laban heard that Jacob had left.
2. God warned Laban not to harm Jacob.
3. Jacob had been a very faithful shepherd.
4. Laban wanted Leah and Rachel to return with him.
5. Jacob and Laban made a treaty of peace.

III. Who said to whom? (Review section 3, pages 90 to 92.)
   1. "Say unto Esau that I have returned and that I have a rich present for him."
   2. "When Esau asks who you are and to whom the camels belong, say that they are a present to him from Jacob."
   3. "Your brother, Esau, is coming."
   4. "I have enough, my brother. Keep what is yours."
   5. "God has been very generous with me, and I am happy to share my wealth with my brother."

IV. Questions for discussion:
   1. Compare Laban and Esau.
   2. What other Bible stories tell about a quarrel between brothers or relatives? Did the story end happily or unhappily?

THINGS TO DO

1. *Radio Play*—Read "Reunion with Esau" as if it were a radio play. The following parts are needed: narrator, Jacob, messengers, servants, Esau. (The first and second sections about the flight from Laban might also be read as a radio play.)

2. *Original Story*—Write a story for your class newspaper about two brothers. Let the story end happily.

A LETTER GAME

Call out a letter and something about the name it stands for; for example "C—a country." The student must then guess that C stands for Canaan. The class may be divided into 2 or more teams.

UNIT FOUR

Joseph and His Brothers

CHAPTER X

JOSEPH THE DREAMER

1. TWO DREAMS

WHEN JACOB returned to Canaan a sad thing happened—his beloved wife, Rachel, died. Jacob sadly buried Rachel near the city of Bethlehem.

Rachel was the mother of two sons, Joseph and Benjamin. Jacob now showed great love for Joseph, the son of Rachel. The other brothers became very jealous of Joseph, especially when Jacob made him a beautiful coat of many colors.

Once Joseph dreamed a dream.

"Listen to what I dreamed," he said with a smile to his brothers. "I dreamed that we were in the field, and your sheaves of grain bowed down to my sheaf."

"What does this mean?" said the brothers angrily. "Do you think that you will rule over us, and that we will bow down to you?"

A little while later Joseph said, "I dreamed another dream. This time I dreamed that the sun, the moon and eleven stars bowed down to me."

Even Jacob became angry.

"Do you think that your parents and your eleven brothers will bow down to you?"

Joseph's brothers began to hate him, but Jacob thought to himself, "Perhaps these dreams really have some special meaning."

2. REVENGE

One day Jacob called to Joseph and said, "Your brothers are taking care of the sheep in Shechem. Go and see whether all is well with them."

Shechem was a long distance from Hebron where Jacob lived. Joseph went in search of his brothers.

His brothers saw him while he was still far off. One of the brothers said, "Look, here comes the dreamer."

"Let's take revenge for those silly dreams," said a second brother. "He thinks he's better than we are."

The brothers became more and more angry as they talked about Joseph. Reuben, the oldest brother, was afraid they might do real harm to Joseph.

"Let us not touch him," said Reuben. "We do not want to shed blood. Let's just throw him into a pit. At least we won't be guilty of taking his life."

"That's a good plan," they agreed.

Reuben's real plan was to come back later and to help Joseph out of the pit.

As soon as Joseph drew near, they seized him, removed his coat of many colors, and threw him into a dried-up well.

Reuben left for a little while to feed his sheep. Meanwhile, a camel caravan of Midianite merchants passed by.

Judah, another brother, thought that this would be a good opportunity to save Joseph's life. He turned to his brothers and said, "Why should we slay our brother? If we leave him in the pit he will die. Let's sell him as a slave to these merchants. After all, he is our own flesh and blood."

The brothers agreed. They drew up Joseph from the pit and sold him as a slave for twenty pieces of silver.

A short time later Reuben went to the pit to save Joseph. When he saw that the pit was empty he ran to his brothers to find out what had happened. When they told him what they had done, he cried out, "What shall I do? I am the oldest and our father will blame me."

"Our father does not have to know," said another brother. "Let us dip Joseph's coat in the blood of a goat, and our father will think that Joseph was slain by a wild beast."

The brothers slew a goat, and dipped Joseph's coat of many colors in the blood.

They brought the coat to Jacob and said, "This is what we found. We do not know whether it is your son's coat or not."

Jacob examined the coat and said, "It is my son's coat. A wild beast has killed him. Joseph is dead! My son is dead!"

Jacob wept bitterly for many days. His sons and his daughter tried to comfort him, but Jacob continued to mourn.

"Joseph is dead! My son is dead!" he wept. "I shall mourn for him until the day that I go to my own grave!"

3. IN THE LAND OF EGYPT

Meanwhile the Midianite merchants brought Joseph to Egypt. There they sold Joseph as a slave to Potiphar, the captain of the king's guard.

Potiphar noticed how clever Joseph was in all that he did. Soon Potiphar became rich because of Joseph's wise help.

Potiphar was very much pleased with Joseph.

"You will be overseer in my house," said Potiphar to Joseph. "From now on you will be in charge of my entire household."

Joseph took care of all of Potiphar's affairs, and he succeeded in all of his work.

But Potiphar's wife fell in love with Joseph. When Joseph refused to return her love she became very angry.

"Joseph is not a faithful servant," she said to Potiphar. "I demand that he be placed in prison."

Potiphar did not know that his wife was telling a lie. He placed poor Joseph in prison as his wife demanded.

But even in prison Joseph succeeded. The keeper of the prison began to trust Joseph with many important duties.

"I place all the prisoners in your hands," said the keeper of the prison. "You are in charge."

Joseph now took care of all prison affairs, but he prayed for the day when he would be free once more.

EXERCISES

I. Answer each question in a complete sentence. (Review section 1, pages 97 to 98.)
  1. Where was Rachel buried?
  2. What special gift did Jacob give to Joseph?
  3. What did Joseph dream in his first dream?
  4. Who bowed down to Joseph's star in the second dream?
  5. Why were the brothers angry at Joseph?

II. Complete each sentence. (Review section 2, pages 98 to 100.)

   JACOB, JOSEPH, JUDAH, MIDIANITES, REUBEN
  1. _____ went to find his brothers in Shechem.
  2. _____ said, "We do not want to shed blood. Let's just throw him into a pit."
  3. _____ tried to save his brother's life by saying he should be sold as a slave.
  4. The _____ bought Joseph as a slave for twenty pieces of silver.
  5. _____ thought that Joseph was killed by a wild beast.

III. Choose the correct phrase or name. (Review section 3, page 100.)
  1. Joseph became a slave in _____. (Egypt, Syria)
  2. Joseph was sold as a slave by the _____. (Midianites, Philistines)
  3. Joseph was overseer in the house of _____. (Potiphar, Pharaoh)
  4. Joseph was placed in prison because of Potiphar's _____. (daughter, wife)

5. Joseph was placed in charge of the prisoners by the _____. (captain of the guard, keeper of the prison)

IV. Questions for discussion:
1. Did Reuben do the right thing when he suggested that Joseph be thrown into the pit?
2. What other stories about dreams do you know? Did the dream come true?

THINGS TO DO

1. *Research*—How are the names of Jacob's children pronounced? You may consult the *Guide to Pronunciation*, beginning on page 205.

Jacob had 12 sons: Reuben, Simeon, Levi, Judah, Zebulun, Issachar, Dan, Gad, Asher, Naphtali, Joseph, Benjamin.

Jacob had one daughter named Dinah.

2. *Assembly Program*—Plan a program for the school assembly based on the story of Joseph. You may use a printed play found in a book in your school library, or you may write your own play.

MEMORY QUIZ

Study the names of Jacob's children for 5 minutes; then see how many you can repeat.

CHAPTER XI

FROM PRISON TO PRIME MINISTER

1. THE BUTLER AND THE BAKER

ONE DAY Joseph was placed in charge of two new prisoners. Both men had been officers in the court of Pharaoh, king of Egypt. One man was the butler who had served wine to the king; the other man was the king's baker.

Nobody was sure why these men were placed in prison. Some people said they were suspected of trying to poison Pharaoh. There was also a rumor that a fly had been found in the king's wine, and a pebble in the king's bread.

Joseph took good care of these two prisoners. One night both the butler and the baker dreamed strange dreams. Each one told his dream to the other prisoners, but nobody knew the meaning of their dreams.

When Joseph saw them in the morning he noticed how sad they were.

"Why do you look so sad?" asked Joseph.

"We have dreamed strange dreams," they replied, "and nobody can explain the meaning of the dreams."

"Tell me what you dreamed," said Joseph. "Maybe God will help to make clear the real explanation of your dreams."

"This was my dream," said the butler. "In my dream I saw a vine with three branches. On the branches were ripe grapes. Pharaoh's cup was in my hand. And I took the grapes and pressed them into Pharaoh's cup, and I gave the cup to Pharaoh to drink."

"This is the meaning of your dream," said Joseph. "The three branches are three days. In three more days Pharaoh will free you from prison and restore you to your position as king's butler."

"You are indeed a wise man," said the butler. "How can I reward you for explaining the meaning of my dream?"

"You can do me a great favor," said Joseph, "by asking Pharaoh to release me from prison. I was stolen out of the land of the Hebrews, and I was later placed in prison although I had done nothing wrong."

"I shall surely remember you when Pharaoh restores me to office," said the butler.

When the chief baker heard Joseph's explanation, he said, "Perhaps you can explain the meaning of my dream."

"I shall try," said Joseph.

"In my dream," said the baker, "I saw three white baskets on my head. In the top basket was baked food which the birds ate."

"The three baskets are three days. In three days, Pharaoh will hang you on a tree and the birds will devour your flesh."

Pharaoh soon found out that the butler was innocent, but that the baker was guilty. Three days later he restored the butler to his office, but the baker was hanged.

But the butler forgot his promise and did not mention Joseph's name to Pharaoh.

2. PHARAOH'S DREAM

Two years passed by and Joseph was still in prison.

One night Pharaoh dreamed a dream which frightened him. He awoke in the middle of the night and wondered about his dream. Then he fell asleep again and dreamed a second dream.

The next morning he called his wise men to him. "You must explain the meanings of these two dreams," said Pharaoh. "I cannot rest until I receive a clear explanation."

The wise men listened, but they were puzzled. They did not know what to say to Pharaoh.

At that moment the chief butler came to the king and said, "I know one man who can help you."

"Who is he?" asked Pharaoh. "Hurry and bring him to me."

"His name is Joseph," said the butler, "and he is a prisoner in the king's dungeon. Two years ago when the baker and I were in prison, we dreamed strange dreams which Joseph explained to us. Every word of his came true."

Pharaoh quickly sent for Joseph who was brought before him.

And Pharaoh said, "I have dreamed a dream, but none

can explain its meaning to me. I have been told that you are able to explain all dreams. If so, I shall reward you greatly."

"Explanations belong to God," replied Joseph. "With His help I shall do my best to give you a truthful answer."

"This is my dream," said Pharaoh. "As I stood near the bank of the Nile River, I saw seven fat, healthy cows come up out of the river. They fed in the grass near the river, but soon seven lean, skinny cows came out of the river and ate up the fat cows." Pharaoh paused for a moment.

"Was this your entire dream?" asked Joseph.

"No," answered Pharaoh. "At first, I woke up after this dream. But then I fell asleep again and dreamed a second dream. This time I dreamed that I was in the field. And I noticed a stalk that had seven ears of corn. The ears were full and good. But then seven thin, withered ears sprang up on the stalk and swallowed the good ears of corn. This was the end of my dream."

And Joseph said to Pharaoh, "God has told you by means of this dream what will happen in the future. The seven fat cows stand for seven years of plenty, and the seven lean cows stand for seven years of famine. There will be seven years of plenty with rich crops, followed by seven years of famine when the crops will be destroyed."

"What is the meaning of the second dream?" asked Pharaoh.

"The second dream is the same as the first," replied Joseph. "The seven full ears of corn stand for seven prosperous years, and the seven thin ears stand for seven years of hardship. This double dream is a special warning to you to save your people from famine and from suffering."

"O wise young man," said Pharaoh, "advise me. What shall I do now?"

"Appoint an officer," said Joseph, "who will be in charge of storing away food. During the seven years of plenty, food must be stored away throughout the land of Egypt. Then when the years of famine come, there will be food to eat. In this way your people will be saved and none will die."

"You shall be in charge," said Pharaoh, "for there is nobody who is wiser than you. Indeed, you will be my prime minister, second only to the king. And you will rule over all Egypt."

3. JOSEPH AS PRIME MINISTER

Pharaoh set Joseph over Egypt as his prime minister. He took the signet ring from his hand and gave it unto Joseph. The king clothed Joseph in special garments of fine linen as a sign of his noble rank, and Joseph rode in the second chariot after the king.

Joseph was thirty years old when he became prime minister. He soon married a girl of noble family. Two sons, named Manasseh and Ephraim, were born to him.

It was a very great honor to be prime minister of Egypt, for Egypt was then the greatest country in the world. Egypt was the first country to construct a calendar, to make paper, or to plow with oxen. More than a thousand years before Joseph, the kings of Egypt built giant pyramids in the desert that are still the wonder of the world.

Through the land of Egypt flowed the Nile River. Each year the river overflowed its banks and the farmers planted seeds in the rich soil.

The farmers would count the days each year waiting for the Nile to rise. They knew that 365 days passed between one overflow of the river and the next overflow. That is how the people of Egypt were the first to discover that there were 365 days in the year.

When the harvest season came Joseph sent officers to each section of Egypt.

"We come in the name of Pharaoh and of his Prime Minister, Joseph," said the officers.

"What do you want of us?" asked the farmers.

"One part in every five of your crops you must give to Pharaoh," said the officers. "Four parts in five you may keep for yourselves."

At first the farmers complained; but when they saw how rich the crop was they paid one part in five, and there was still food in abundance.

Year after year the golden grain danced in the sun. Never had the farmers seen such plenty. Joseph's officers stored away grain until there was no longer any space in the storehouses. For seven years the plenty continued.

Then after seven years the Nile River failed to rise beyond its banks. The fields were dry and the seeds rotted in the earth.

"We will die of hunger," shouted the farmers. "The land has been cursed."

"None will go hungry," said Joseph to the people. "You may go to Pharaoh's storehouses for food."

The storehouses were opened, and the people received food and they ate.

Joseph's words had come true. Through his wisdom he had saved the Egyptian nation.

EXERCISES

I. The butler or the baker? (Review section 1, pages 103 to 105.)
   1. The _____ dreamed that he saw a vine with three branches.
   2. The _____ dreamed that the birds ate the food in the upper basket.
   3. The _____ promised to help free Joseph from prison.
   4. After three days the _____ was restored to his former position.
   5. After three days the _____ was hanged.

II. True or false? (Review section 2, pages 105 to 107.)
   1. The baker told Pharaoh about Joseph.
   2. Pharaoh dreamed that the seven fat cows ate the seven lean cows.
   3. Pharaoh's second dream was about seven ears of corn.
   4. Joseph said that the seven lean years would be followed by seven years of plenty.
   5. Joseph became prime minister of Egypt.

110   HEROES OF JEWISH HISTORY

III. Fill in the correct number. (Review section 3, pages 107 to 109.)
1. Joseph was _____ years old when he became prime minister.
2. Joseph had _____ sons.
3. The pyramids had been built _____ years before Joseph.
4. _____ days passed between one overflow of the Nile and the next overflow.
5. The farmers paid in taxes one part in _____.
6. There were _____ years of plenty.

IV. Questions for discussion:
1. What did Egypt contribute to the world?
2. How is famine prevented today?

THINGS TO DO

1. *Research*—Bring in a report on one of the following topics dealing with Egypt: *a*—the Nile River, *b*—the pyramids, *c*—Egyptian writing.
2. *Puppets*—Dramatize the Joseph story through the use of puppets. A simple puppet can be made by fashioning the head out of a bag filled with newspapers. A stick can serve as the body.

PUZZLE

Answer the following questions. The initial letters of the answers will spell out the name of one of Jacob's sons.
1. What is the capital of Israel?
2. What was Abraham to Lot?
3. What did Joseph interpret for Pharaoh?
4. What nation was descended from Ishmael?
5. Where is the field of Machpelah?

CHAPTER XII

JOSEPH AND BENJAMIN

1. JOSEPH'S BROTHERS IN EGYPT

IN THE LAND of Canaan, too, there was famine, for no rain came down from heaven to water the soil.

When Jacob heard that there was corn to buy in Egypt, he called his sons saying, "I have heard that there is corn in Egypt. Go down to Egypt and buy food so that we may be saved from death."

Jacob did not send Benjamin, Joseph's youngest brother, for fear that an accident might happen to him.

As soon as Joseph saw his brothers he recognized them, but they did not recognize him. When the brothers bowed low before him, Joseph thought of the dreams he had dreamed. For these dreams had indeed come true.

"Where are you from?" asked Joseph.

"We have come from the land of Canaan to buy food," they replied.

"How do I know that you are not spies?" asked Joseph in a harsh voice.

"We are honest men," they said. "We are not spies."

"I do not believe you," said Joseph. "What family do you belong to? Who else is in your family?"

"We are twelve sons of one father in Canaan," said the brothers.

"I count only ten," said Joseph. "Where are the other two?"

"Our youngest brother remained in Canaan," they said, "and one is no longer alive."

"You are surely spies who have come to spy out the weak spots in Egypt," said Joseph.

Joseph kept the brothers for three days. After the third day he said, "If you wish to prove to me that you are not spies, bring your youngest brother with you when you come again to buy corn. In the meanwhile you may return so that your families will have food, and will not die from famine."

The brothers were greatly frightened.

"This has all happened," said Reuben, "as a punishment for what we did to our brother. Did I not plead with you not to harm him?"

Reuben spoke in Hebrew to his brothers. He did not know that Joseph understood each word, for before this they had spoken to Joseph by means of an interpreter.

Joseph then took Simeon, who had led the brothers in plotting against him, and kept him in Egypt as a hostage. He commanded his servants to give the brothers corn, and to replace their money in their sacks.

On the way back one of the brothers opened his sack and found the money.

"This is a terrible thing," said the brothers in fear, "for now the man will say that we stole the money."

When the brothers came to Canaan they sadly told Jacob what had happened. Meanwhile each man opened his sack and found the money in the mouth of the sack.

"What will happen to us now?" they asked in great fright.

"Benjamin will never go with you," said Jacob angrily. "Joseph is dead and Simeon is in prison, and now you want to take Benjamin too. If anything happens to Benjamin, you will bring down my gray hairs with sorrow unto the grave."

2. THE SECOND JOURNEY TO EGYPT

When all the corn had been eaten up, Jacob said to his sons, "Go again and buy us some food."

And Judah said, "How can we go unless you send Benjamin too? The man clearly said that we cannot see his face again unless we bring our younger brother with us."

"Why did you tell him you have another brother?" asked Jacob.

"We could not help it. He asked us questions about the other members of our family. But have no fear. I shall be responsible for Benjamin, and I promise you that he will return safely."

"If it must be so," said Jacob, "carry a special present to the man of the fruits of Canaan. Bring honey and spices and nuts and almonds. Take along a double sum of money, and return the money you found in your sacks. I pray unto

God that He will protect Benjamin and that the man will deal kindly with you."

When the brothers arrived in Egypt they were told that Joseph wanted them to dine in his house. At first the brothers thought they were to be punished because of the money they had found in their sacks.

"We did not take the money," they said to the steward of Joseph's house. "We found the money in our sacks and do not know who put it there."

"Peace be to you," said the steward; "fear not. It was not our money." He also brought out Simeon to them.

When Joseph came home the brothers gave him the present.

And Joseph asked, "Is your father well? Is he yet alive?"

"Our father is well; he is yet alive," they said.

Joseph then saw Benjamin, his youngest brother. "Is this your youngest brother of whom you spoke?"

"It is," said the brothers.

"May God bless you," said Joseph to Benjamin.

Joseph could no longer control his great joy at seeing his beloved brother. He quickly retired to his room and wept tears of gladness that he was able to see his brother. But when he returned he said nothing to his brothers.

3. THE SILVER CUP

The brothers ate in silence wondering why they had been honored by the Egyptians. Each brother was placed at the table in accordance with his age; Reuben was placed

JOSEPH AND HIS BROTHERS

in the first seat and Benjamin in the last. The brothers could not understand who had found out their ages.

Meanwhile Joseph gave orders to his steward to place his silver cup in Benjamin's sack. When the brothers departed, Joseph ordered the steward to pursue after them. Joseph really planned to see how loyal the brothers would be to Benjamin.

"Why did you steal my lord's silver cup?" said the steward to the brothers.

"Far be it from us to do such a thing," said the brothers. "If any man has done this we will all be your slaves."

"Only the one who has sinned will be punished," replied the steward.

He examined their sacks and found the silver cup in Benjamin's sack.

Frightened and silent the brothers returned to Joseph.

"The man who is guilty shall be my slave," said Joseph. "The rest of you may return to your father."

Then Judah came near and said, "Let me be a slave in place of my brother. If we do not bring him back, his father will die. He warned us that if anything happened to his youngest son, we would bring down his gray hairs with sorrow unto the grave. I swore that I would be responsible. Let me therefore be the slave, and send my brother back to Canaan."

Joseph could no longer restrain himself.

"Come near to me," he said to his brothers. "I am Joseph your brother! I am your long-lost brother, Joseph!"

Joseph embraced his brother Benjamin and wept. He

kissed his brothers and said, "Do not fear because you sold me as a slave. It was the will of God so that I could save your lives and the lives of this whole nation, for the famine will continue for five more years."

The brothers rejoiced that their brother was still alive and that their sin had been pardoned.

EXERCISES

I. Who said to whom? (Review section 1, pages 111 to 113.)
  1. "Go down to Egypt and buy food so that we may be saved from death."
  2. "We are honest men. We are not spies."
  3. "You are surely spies who have come to spy out the weak spots in Egypt."
  4. "This has all happened as a punishment for what we did to our brother."
  5. "Joseph is dead and Simeon is in prison, and now you want to take Benjamin too."

II. Answer each question in a complete sentence. (Review section 2, pages 113 to 114.)
  1. Who promised to take care of Benjamin?
  2. What present did the brothers bring to Joseph?
  3. Where did the brothers dine?
  4. What did the steward say to the brothers?
  5. Why did Joseph weep?

III. Match: (Review section 3, pages 114 to 117.)

Column A	Column B
Benjamin	1. offered to remain a slave in Egypt.
Joseph	2. was released from prison.
Judah	3. ruled over Egypt.
Reuben	4. was accused of stealing the silver cup.
Simeon	5. was the oldest brother.

IV. Questions for discussion:
1. Should Joseph have told immediately that he was their brother?
2. Who was the leader among the eleven brothers? What proof do you have?

THINGS TO DO

1. *Research*—The Siddur or prayer-book often refers to "God of Abraham, God of Isaac, and God of Jacob." Bring in the exact words of a paragraph in which this phrase is found.

2. *The Twelve Tribes and their Symbols*—The sons of Jacob were ancestors of the 12 tribes. There was a special flag for each tribe. Draw a poster or design for one of the tribes including the special symbol.

Here are the symbols of the tribes:

Reuben—Mandrakes (a plant formed like a little man) on a red flag
Simeon—A fortified city on a green flag
Judah—A lion on an azure flag
Issachar—The sun and the moon on a black flag
Zebulun—A ship on a white flag
Dan—A serpent on a sapphire blue flag

Gad—A camp on a red and black flag
Naphtali—A gazelle on a wine-red flag
Asher—An olive tree on a fiery red flag
Ephraim—A bull on a black flag
Manasseh—A unicorn on a black flag
Benjamin—A wolf on a flag containing the colors of all the other flags

(One of Jacob's sons, Levi, is not counted among the twelve tribes since the descendants of Levi served in the Temple or were teachers scattered throughout the Land of Israel. Joseph had two shares since both his sons were included among the tribes.)

THE LION OF JUDAH GAME

Draw a lion to represent the lion of Judah. See who can come closest when blindfolded to placing the tail on the lion.

CHAPTER XIII

REUNION IN EGYPT

1. JACOB IN EGYPT

WHEN PHARAOH heard that Joseph's brothers were in Egypt he was very much pleased.

"Tell your brothers to bring your father and their families to Egypt," said Pharaoh to Joseph." They may take wagons from Egypt in which to carry all their belongings."

Joseph repeated Pharaoh's words to his brothers. "Tell our father," added Joseph, "that I am lord of Egypt. Let him be near me, and I will take care of him and his family."

Joseph gave a present to each brother, but to Benjamin he gave a special present of 300 shekels of silver and five changes of clothing.

When the brothers arrived in Canaan, they told the good news to Jacob.

"Joseph is still alive," they said. "We saw him in Egypt."

Jacob's heart missed a beat. He could hardly believe what they said.

"My son is still alive?" he asked.

"He is alive and well. He is ruler over all the land of Egypt."

When Jacob saw the wagons and the presents he knew that they spoke the truth.

"It is enough," said Jacob. "Joseph my son is yet alive! I will go and see him before I die!"

Jacob and his children and grandchildren traveled to Goshen in Egypt where they were met by Joseph. When Joseph saw Jacob he kissed his father and they wept.

"Joseph my son, my son," said Jacob. "At last I have seen you again. Now I can die happy, I have seen that you are still alive!"

2. THE DEATH OF JACOB

Jacob lived in Goshen in the land of Egypt for seventeen years. He was very proud of Joseph's two sons, Manasseh and Ephraim, and said they would be equal with his own sons.

"In days to come," said Jacob, "when a father wishes to bless his son he will say 'May God make you like Ephraim and Manasseh'."

Before his death Jacob called his twelve sons together and gave each son a special blessing. Jacob's sons became the ancestors of the twelve tribes of Israel.

When Jacob died at a ripe old age he was buried in the field of Machpelah next to Leah. It was the same burial-place in which his parents, Isaac and Rebecca, and his grandparents, Abraham and Sarah, had been buried.

Pharaoh ordered that all Egypt mourn for this great man after his death.

Jacob was the last of the three great ancestors of the Hebrew people. He was the father of the twelve tribes of Israel. His special name, Israel, became the name of Canaan for in later years the name was changed to the Land of Israel. The Hebrew people were often called children of Israel or Israelites.

On May 14, 1948 when a Jewish state was established the founders of the state proudly chose the name Israel as the name of this new state.

3. THE LAST YEARS OF JOSEPH

Joseph continued to rule wisely over the land of Egypt. For five more years, during the famine, he fed the people of Egypt with bread.

"You have saved our lives," said the people of Egypt.

Even after the famine was over the people continued to pay Pharaoh one part in five of all that they harvested.

The brothers of Joseph were greatly afraid after the death of Jacob.

"Perhaps Joseph will punish us now because we sold him into slavery. Maybe he was only kind to us while Jacob was alive."

The brothers decided to send a message to Joseph.

"Our father Jacob commanded that you pardon our sin. These were his words before his death."

Joseph called his brothers to him. They appeared before him and bowed low to the ground.

"We are your servants," they said.

"Rise," said Joseph. "Fear not. Although you sold me as a slave, it was really God's will. In this way I was able to save many people from death. You and your little ones may remain in Egypt, and I shall help you."

His brothers saw how kind Joseph really was, and they knew there was nothing to fear. They lived in peace in Goshen where there was good pasture land for their sheep.

When Joseph was old he called the children of Israel to him.

"I am about to die," said Joseph. "I know that God will keep his promise and bring you up out of this land to the land which He promised to Abraham, Isaac and Jacob."

"We will never forget God's promise," said the children of Israel.

"And now swear to me," said Joseph, "that when you return to Canaan you will bring up my last remains with you. Swear that you will bury my bones in the land of my fathers."

"We swear," said the children of Israel.

And Joseph died at the age of 110, and he was mourned by all Egypt and by the children of Israel.

EXERCISES

I. Choose the correct name. (Review section 1, pages 120 to 121.)

1. _____said that the children of Israel could use

wagons to carry their goods to Egypt. (Pharaoh, Jacob)
2. _____ promised to take care of Jacob in Egypt. (Judah, Joseph)
3. _____ was given a special present by Joseph. (Benjamin, Reuben)
4. Jacob at first could not believe that _____ was still alive. (Joseph, Simeon)
5. Jacob was reunited with Joseph in _____. (Egypt, Canaan)

II. Complete each sentence. (Review section 2, pages 121 to 122.)

Israel, Jacob, Leah, Manasseh, Pharaoh

1. Fathers bless their sons by saying, "May God make you like Ephraim and _____."
2. Jacob was buried in the field of Machpelah next to _____.
3. _____ ordered that all Egypt mourn for Jacob.
4. _____, or Israel, was the father of the twelve tribes of Israel.
5. 1948 marks the beginning of the state of _____.

III. True or false? (Review section 3, pages 122 to 123.)

1. When the years of famine were over, the people no longer paid taxes to Pharaoh.
2. The brothers were afraid that Joseph might punish them after Jacob's death.
3. Joseph said, "Fear not. Although you sold me as a slave, it was really God's will."
4. The children of Israel expected to remain in Egypt forever.
5. Joseph made the children of Israel swear that they would bring back his bones to Canaan.

IV. Questions for discussion:
   1. Why is Jacob important in Jewish history?
   2. Some people think that the story of Joseph is the best story in the Bible. Do you agree or disagree? Why?

REVIEW QUESTIONS

for Units Three and Four (pages 71 to 125)

1. In what ways does the story of Jacob and Esau resemble the story of Joseph and his brothers?
2. Tell about the following dreams:
   a. Jacob's dream at Beth-El
   b. Joseph's dreams
   c. The butler's dream
   d. The baker's dream
   e. Pharaoh's dreams
3. Write a sentence about each of the following:
   Isaac, Rebecca, Jacob, Esau, Haran, Rachel, Laban, Leah, Bethlehem, Joseph, Midianites, Potiphar, the butler, the baker, Pharaoh, Reuben, Simeon, Judah, Benjamin, Goshen.

TEST

on Units Three and Four

I. Complete each sentence. (25 points)
   1. _____ dreamed that angels climbed up and down the ladder reaching from the earth to heaven.

2. _____ dreamed that the sun, moon and eleven stars bowed down to his star.
3. The _____ dreamed that he pressed the grapes from the three branches into Pharaoh's cup.
4. The _____ dreamed that the birds ate food from the upper basket on his head.
5. _____ dreamed that the seven lean cows ate the seven fat cows.

II. Choose the correct word or name. (25 points)
1. The Philistines quarreled with Isaac about (sheep, silver, wells).
2. Esau sold Jacob his (birthright, blessing, field).
3. Laban lived in (Haran, Hebron, Ur).
4. Joseph was the son of (Leah, Rachel, Rebecca).
5. "I shall be a slave in place of Benjamin," said (Judah, Reuben, Simeon).

III. Why? (30 points)
1. Why did Jacob run away to Haran?
2. Why did Jacob serve Laban for 20 years?
3. Why did the brothers hate Joseph?
4. Why did Jacob refuse to send Benjamin to Egypt?
5. Why did Joseph take one part in five from each farmer?

IV. Match: (20 points)

Column A	*Column B*
Benjamin	1. helped free Joseph from prison.
The butler	2. tried to save Joseph from death.
Jacob	3. was the youngest of twelve brothers.
Laban	4. was the father of the twelve tribes.
Reuben	5. was the father of Rachel and Leah.

UNIT FIVE

Out of the House of Bondage

CHAPTER XIV

MOSES

1. SLAVES IN EGYPT

MANY YEARS passed after the death of Joseph. The children of Israel were very happy in Goshen in the land of Egypt, for there they found green pastures for their sheep and they prospered.

Although they lived in Egypt the children of Israel did not change their customs. They wore the same shepherd costumes that they had worn in Canaan. They gave their children Hebrew names and spoke Hebrew to their children. They believed in one God and did not worship idols as did their Egyptian neighbors.

After many, many years there arose a new king who did not remember Joseph. He did not know that once a Hebrew had saved the people of Egypt from famine and from starvation.

The king of Egypt called in his advisers and asked, "How shall we deal with the children of Israel?"

"There are too many of them," said one adviser. "In case of war they might fight on the side of our enemy."

"Some day they might try to escape from Egypt," said another. "We have given them too much freedom. Let us make slaves of them."

The king agreed that it would be wise to makes slaves of the children of Israel. He set overseers, or taskmasters, over the children of Israel.

The taskmasters were very cruel. They used whips to beat the slaves. They forced the slaves to make bricks and to build cities for Pharaoh. They drove the slaves into the fields and made them toil under the boiling sun from sunrise to sunset.

Still the children of Israel grew in numbers. Jacob had come to Egypt with a handful of people, seventy in all. Now their number had risen into the thousands and hundreds of thousands.

"Slavery is not enough," said Pharaoh. "We must keep their number down."

Again he called his advisers who said, "Let us keep the girls as slaves, but kill the male children."

Pharaoh then commanded, "Every Hebrew son that is born shall be thrown into the river, but every daughter shall be saved alive."

2. THE BIRTH OF MOSES

At that time a son was born to Amram of the tribe of Levi and to his wife, Jochebed. The parents hid the child for three months.

"What shall we do?" said Jochebed to her husband. "Pharaoh's officers will find the child and kill him."

PHARAOH'S DAUGHTER AND MOSES

"We cannot hide him any longer," replied Amram. "We must find some way of saving his life."

"Let us place him in a basket near the bank of the river," said Jochebed. "Maybe a kind Egyptian will find him and take care of him."

Amram and his wife took reeds from the river's edge and made a small ark or basket. They smeared the basket with slime and black pitch, and placed the baby in the basket of bulrushes or reeds.

Jochebed called her daughter, Miriam, and said, "Miriam, you must stand near the basket and watch to see who will find the baby."

They put the basket in the reeds near the edge of the river and left Miriam to watch over the child.

Each day, Pharaoh's daughter came down to the Nile River to bathe in its waters. As Pharaoh's daughter walked along the bank of the river with her maidens, she saw the basket of bulrushes.

"Fetch that basket," said Pharaoh's daughter to one of the maidens. "Let us see what is in it."

They brought the basket and opened it. Inside was a baby that cried and cried.

"What a pretty baby!" said Pharaoh's daughter. "It must be a Hebrew child. It's a shame to let it cry this way. Let's find a nurse for it."

Miriam, who stood nearby, heard the words of Pharaoh's daughter.

"I know a very good nurse," said Miriam. "She is one of the Hebrew women, and she will take very good care of the child."

"Thank you," said Pharaoh's daughter. "Please go and call her."

Miriam ran and told her mother what had happened. Jochebed quickly came to the river's edge.

"Will you nurse this child for me?" asked Pharaoh's daughter.

"Gladly," said Jochebed.

"I shall pay you good wages," said the princess. "He's a fine lad and I should like to see him well taken care of."

Amram and Jochebed rejoiced that their child had been saved. The mother nursed the boy who grew up alongside of his brother, Aaron, who was three years older, and his sister, Miriam.

From time to time Jochebed brought the child to the palace, to Pharaoh's daughter. The princess was very fond of the child and called him Moses which means "drawn out of the water," for she had saved him from the river.

There is a very pretty legend told about the infant Moses and Pharaoh. Once when Moses played in the palace he noticed the glittering crown on the king's head. The child reached out, grasped the golden crown and placed it on his own head.

Pharaoh was very much worried. "Perhaps this is a sign that some day he will really remove my crown and take away my power as king."

"It was only a childish act," said one of Pharaoh's wise men. "Put a glowing coal near the crown, and the child will touch the coal because of the brightness of the flame."

"Let us test him," said Pharaoh. "Bring a hot coal. But

if he touches the crown again I shall put him to death because it is a bad sign."

A glowing coal was brought, but the child still was attracted by the crown. Just as he was about to touch the crown, the legend tells, an angel of God pushed his hand toward the coal. The child quickly put the coal in his mouth.

The child's tongue was badly burnt, and ever after Moses was tongue-tied and spoke with difficulty. But this saved the boy's life, for had he grasped the crown Pharaoh would surely have put him to death.

This story is not found in the Bible. It is only a legend, but it hints at the fact that the day would come when Moses would really deprive Pharaoh of his power.

3. MOSES GROWS UP

When Jochebed stopped nursing Moses, she brought him to the princess to live in the palace. The princess adopted Moses as her own son, and he grew up as an Egyptian prince in the palace of the king.

But Moses never forgot that he was a Hebrew. He was sad when he saw how cruel the Egyptians were to the children of Israel. Moses swore that when he grew up he would help his people.

One day Moses went into the fields.

"I should like to see what I can do to help these poor slaves," he said to himself.

Moses watched the taskmasters as they forced the slaves

to do hard work under the burning sun. Suddenly he saw a taskmaster raise a whip and cruelly beat a Hebrew slave.

"Mercy!" cried the slave. "Have mercy!"

But the taskmaster knew no mercy. Instead he continued to beat the bleeding slave.

Moses could no longer control his anger. He ran to the taskmaster and struck him a heavy blow. The Egyptian fell to the ground.

Moses looked down and was shocked to see that the Egyptian was dead. Quickly Moses buried the body in the sand and went away.

The next day Moses went into the fields once more. As he watched the slaves he heard two Hebrews quarreling. Suddenly one man began to beat the other.

"Why do you beat him?" asked Moses in anger. "Is it not enough that the taskmasters are so cruel? Must the children of Israel be cruel to each other?"

"Who made you a ruler and a judge over us?" said the slave. "Do you think you can kill me the way you killed the Egyptian?"

Moses became greatly troubled when he heard the words of the slave.

"My deed has become known," said Moses. "If Pharaoh hears of it he will be very angry."

The slave's words were reported to the palace. When Pharaoh heard of what Moses had done, he said, "He must pay with his life for killing an Egyptian officer."

The friends of Moses warned him that Pharaoh wanted

to kill him. Moses fled from Egypt and escaped into the land of Midian.

EXERCISES

I. Arrange the following sentences in the order in which these things happened. (Review section 1, pages 129 to 130.)
1. Pharaoh commanded that every male child be thrown into the river.
2. Joseph died and was mourned by all Egypt.
3. The taskmasters were very cruel to the slaves.
4. A new king arose who did not remember Joseph.
5. The king made slaves of the children of Israel.

II. Who said to whom? (Review section 2, pages 130 to 134.)
1. "We cannot hide him any longer."
2. "Let us place him in a basket near the bank of the river."
3. "Fetch that basket! Let us see what is in it."
4. "I know a very good nurse. She is one of the Hebrew women, and she will take very good care of the child."
5. "Will you nurse this child for me?"

III. Answer each question in a complete sentence. (Review section 3, pages 134 to 136.)
1. Who adopted Moses?
2. Why was Moses sad?
3. What did the taskmaster do to the slave?
4. Why did Moses scold the Hebrew slave?
5. Why did Moses escape to Midian?

IV. Questions for discussion:
   1. What did Moses learn in the home of his parents that helped him become a leader of the Hebrew people? What did he learn in the palace that helped him become a leader?
   2. Compare the life of the slaves in Egypt with the life of the Negro slaves in America.

THINGS TO DO

1. *Newspaper Report*—Pretend you are a newspaper reporter in the palace of Pharaoh. Write a newspaper story called "I was there." Tell about the following:

(a) The conference at which it was decided to make slaves of the Hebrews. *(b)* The conference at which it was decided to throw the sons into the river. *(c)* The excitement in the palace over the finding of Moses. *(d)* Moses as a young man in the palace. *(e)* The report that Moses had killed an Egyptian.

2. *Spiritual*—Play a phonograph record of the spiritual "Let My People Go."

FLASH-CARD GAME

Prepare questions in Jewish history on flash-cards. The person who answers the question correctly receives the card. The class may be divided into rows or into two teams. The team receiving the greater number of cards is declared the winner.

CHAPTER XV

"LET MY PEOPLE GO"

1. MOSES IN MIDIAN

WHEN MOSES came to the land of Midian, he sat down to rest near a well.

He looked up and saw seven girls approaching with their sheep. Moses watched as the girls drew the water from the well and filled the troughs for the sheep to drink.

Just then shepherds came and roughly pushed away the seven girls. The men began to water their sheep from the troughs that had been filled by the girls.

Moses grew very angry when he saw what the shepherds had done.

"Why do you do such a selfish and unkind thing?" shouted Moses.

He ran to the shepherds, lifted his stick and drove the men away. Then he helped the girls water the flock.

"Thank you for your kindness," said the girls. "We are the seven daughters of Jethro. Each day the shepherds drive us away, and we are not strong enough to protect ourselves."

The girls then returned to their home.

When Jethro, their father, saw them he said, "You have come back very early. How is it that you returned so soon today?"

"An Egyptian protected us from the shepherds and helped us water the flock," said the daughters.

"Where is this kind man?" asked Jethro.

"He remained near the well," they replied.

"Why did you leave him there? Call him so that he may eat bread and rest."

The daughters called Moses who came to Jethro's home. Moses stayed with Jethro and took care of his sheep.

Moses married Zipporah, the daughter of Jethro, and was very happy in Midian.

But Moses never forgot the Hebrew slaves in Egypt. "If only I could help them!" he thought to himself.

One day Jethro said, "I have heard that the king of Egypt is dead, and a new Pharaoh is on the throne. Now you do not have to fear that he will seek to kill you."

"Maybe the new king will be kinder to the slaves," said Moses.

Moses knew in his heart that some day he would have to return to Egypt to help free the children of Israel.

There is a pretty legend which says that one day a sheep ran away from the flock. Moses ran after the sheep, and overtook it near a stream of water. The sheep bent down to drink.

"Poor sheep," said Moses. "You were thirsty and I did not know it."

Moses tenderly lifted the sheep and carried it back to the flock.

At that moment, God said, "Moses, Moses, you have been a kind shepherd to the sheep. I have picked you, therefore, to be the leader and shepherd of my people Israel."

2. THE BURNING BUSH

One day as Moses led the flock to the edge of the wilderness, he came to the foot of Mount Sinai.

An angel of God appeared to Moses in a flame of fire in a thorn bush. Moses looked up and saw the bush on fire, but to his surprise the burning bush was not consumed by the fire.

"I shall turn aside and see this wonderful thing," said Moses. "Why isn't the bush burnt?"

And God called unto Moses and said, "Moses, Moses."

"Here am I," said Moses.

"Do not come any nearer," said God. "Remove your shoes from your feet, for the place on which you stand is holy ground."

Then God said, "I am the God of your fathers, the God of Abraham, the God of Isaac and the God of Jacob. I have heard the cry of the children of Israel. I shall deliver them out of the hand of the Egyptians, and bring them to a land flowing with milk and with honey. Come now, therefore, and go unto Pharaoh, and bring forth the children of Israel out of Egypt."

And Moses said, "Who am I that I should go to Pharaoh?"

"Do not worry," replied God. "I shall be with you. Gather the elders of Israel and go unto Pharaoh. Say that God has appeared unto you and has ordered you to travel a three days' journey into the wilderness to sacrifice to Him."

"But the people will not believe me. They will say that God did not appear to me. They will ask for a sign."

"Take the rod which is in your hand," said God, "and throw it on the ground."

Moses threw the stick on the ground and it became a serpent.

"Pick it up by the tail."

Moses picked it up by the tail and it became a rod once more.

"This is the sign. And the people will believe you," said God, "when they see the sign."

And Moses said, "O Lord, I am not a man of words. I am slow of speech. Send somebody else."

"Your brother Aaron will be with you," said God. "He speaks well. Teach him what to say and he will be your spokesman unto the people."

Moses returned to Jethro his father-in-law and said, "Let me go back to my brothers in Egypt to see how they are faring. Later my family will join me."

And Jethro said, "Go in peace."

3. MOSES AND AARON BEFORE PHARAOH

Moses met Aaron, his brother, at Mount Sinai. He told him of his mission to Pharaoh.

Then they went to Egypt and gathered the elders of the people.

"God has heard your cries and will deliver you from the hand of Pharaoh," said Moses and Aaron.

When the people saw the rod turn into a serpent and when they heard the words of Moses and Aaron they believed that at last they would be freed from slavery.

Moses and Aaron then went to Pharaoh.

"The Lord, God of Israel, has appeared to us and ordered us to hold a feast unto Him in the wilderness. God says unto you, 'Pharaoh, let My people go!'"

And Pharaoh said, "Who is the Lord that I should listen to His voice? You are just lazy and do not want to work."

Moses and Aaron said, "We will show you a sign." They turned the rod into a serpent but still Pharaoh would not listen to them.

"I do not know the Lord," said Pharaoh.

"Once more we warn you to obey the words of God," said Moses and Aaron. "'Let My people go!'"

"I will not let Israel go," replied Pharaoh.

When Moses and Aaron had left the palace, Pharaoh turned to his officers and said, "We must punish the Hebrew slaves for sending Moses and Aaron to us. From now on we will require more work of them and teach them that Pharaoh will not permit them to be so lazy."

EXERCISES

I. Choose the correct word or name. (Review section 1, pages 138 to 140.)
   1. Moses ran away from Egypt to _____. (Midian, Canaan)
   2. Moses protected the daughters of _____. (Jochebed, Jethro)
   3. Moses married _____. (Dinah, Zipporah)
   4. Moses became a _____. (farmer, shepherd)
   5. God picked Moses to be leader of the children of _____. (Israel, Egypt)

II. Why? (Review section 2, pages 140 to 141.)
   1. Why did Moses go to Mount Sinai?
   2. Why did Moses turn aside to see the bush?
   3. Why did God send Moses to Pharaoh?
   4. Why did Moses ask for a sign?
   5. Why did God decide to send Aaron with Moses?

III. True or false? (Review section 3, page 142.)
   1. Moses met Miriam at Mount Sinai.
   2. The elders of Israel believed the words of Moses and Aaron.
   3. Moses and Aaron appeared before Pharaoh.
   4. Pharaoh said, "I will not let Israel go."
   5. Pharaoh decided to give the slaves less work.

IV. Questions for discussion:
   1. What qualities did Moses show that proved he would make a good leader?
   2. Did Moses ask God to send somebody else because of fear or because of modesty? Prove your statement.

THINGS TO DO

1. *Film*—Show a film or film-strip telling the story of Passover or the story of the children of Israel in Egypt.
2. *Haggadah*—Find a *Haggadah* which contains pictures of the children of Israel in Egypt. Explain each picture to your classmates. (A *Haggadah* is the book used at the *Seder* service on the night of Passover.)

FINISH THE JINGLE

Moses was taken from the water
And saved from death by Pharaoh's _____.

Because he was so kind and brave
He tried to help each Hebrew _____.

The maidens drew from the well so deep
Cool water for their father's _____.

Moses obeyed the Lord's command
And he returned to Egypt _____.

CHAPTER XVI

THE TEN PLAGUES

1. BRICKS WITHOUT STRAW

PHARAOH needed the slaves to build his treasure-cities and his palaces. It had once taken 100,000 men twenty years to build a pyramid. Without the children of Israel he would have to find thousands of slaves elsewhere.

Pharaoh called the taskmasters to him.

"We must teach the children of Israel not to be so lazy," said Pharaoh. "From now on do not give them any straw to make bricks. Let them find their own straw."

"How many bricks shall we require of them?" asked the taskmasters.

"The same number as before, of course."

"But that is impossible," said the taskmasters. "What shall we do if they cannot complete the full number of bricks?"

"Beat them! Take their leaders and whip them! If they weren't so lazy they could do this extra work."

When the taskmasters told the children of Israel that they would not receive straw, the slaves groaned.

"Where shall we get straw?"

"Do not be lazy," said the taskmasters. "Look and you will find."

The slaves scattered throughout the country looking for straw. They found but a few scraps here and there.

When evening fell, the taskmasters called the officers of the children of Israel before them.

"How many bricks have the slaves made?"

"But a few," answered the Hebrew officers. "We cannot make bricks without straw."

The taskmasters raised their whips. "You are too lazy!" they shouted. Again and again they beat the poor slaves until their bodies were but a mass of open sores and bleeding wounds.

The elders of Israel hurried to find Moses and Aaron.

"Is this how you have freed us from slavery? You have just put a sharp sword in the hands of Pharaoh which he uses against us to destroy us."

Moses wept when he heard of the suffering of the slaves.

Moses prayed to God, "Since I have spoken to Pharaoh the suffering of the slaves is too great to bear. Listen to their cries and deliver them!"

And God said, "I shall deliver them with many signs, and wonders, and miracles. Say unto the children of Israel that God has heard their cry and will keep his promise to Abraham, to Isaac and to Jacob."

Moses repeated these words to the children of Israel, but their pain was so great that they grew impatient and would not listen.

SLAVES IN EGYPT

2. THE PLAGUES

God said to Moses and Aaron, "Meet Pharaoh as he goes out to bathe in the Nile River. Say unto him 'Let My people go.' If he refuses lift your rod and the rivers will turn to blood for seven days."

Pharaoh did not even listen to Moses and Aaron. He rudely turned his back and entered his palace.

When the rod was lifted the waters turned red, the color of blood. The Egyptians cried out in horror for there was no water to drink. After seven days the waters became pure once more, and Pharaoh refused to let the people go.

Moses and Aaron returned to the palace of Pharaoh. "Again we warn you to let the people go. If not God will smite all Egypt with the plague of frogs. The river will swarm with frogs which will come into your palace, and into your bedrooms, and into your kitchens. The whole country will be filled with frogs. Only Goshen, where the children of Israel live, will be free of this plague."

When Pharaoh refused, the rod was lifted and Egypt was covered with crawling frogs which crept over the people and into every corner of their houses.

Pharaoh began to weaken. He called for Moses and Aaron in haste and pleaded, "You may go if you want to. Only pray to God to remove the frogs from Egypt."

But as soon as the frogs had disappeared Pharaoh changed his mind and refused to let the people go.

The third plague sent against Egypt was the plague of gnats. The fourth plague was the plague of flies.

The Egyptians stormed the gates of the palace. "How long can we suffer from these plagues?" they shouted.

Pharaoh became frightened when he saw the anger of the people. He called Moses and Aaron and said, "You may sacrifice to God if you want to—but in Egypt."

"God has commanded us to go into the wilderness for this feast."

"I shall allow your people to leave. But do not go far," pleaded Pharaoh.

But as soon as the flies had disappeared Pharaoh forgot his promise and refused to let the people go.

3. THE HARD HEART OF PHARAOH

Moses and Aaron appeared before Pharaoh once more.

"God will send a fifth plague against you because you refuse to let the people of Israel go. A pestilence will attack your cattle, and camels and flocks so that you will not be able to work with your cattle or eat their meat."

But the heart of Pharaoh was hardened and cruel and he refused. After the pestilence there was a sixth plague of boils. A fine dust covered Egypt. As it settled on the people of Egypt it caused boils and skin wounds. This was followed by a seventh plague—the plague of hail.

Moses gave warning to the Egyptians in advance so that the cattle might be saved. Then he stretched forth his rod toward heaven. There was thunder and hail and lightning. The barley and flax crops were then in bloom. The hail came down and ruined the land so that the crops were spoiled.

Pharaoh called to Moses and Aaron. "I have sinned," he said. "I have broken my word. Do not fear. This time I shall let the people of Israel go."

No sooner had the hail ceased than Pharaoh's heart was hardened.

"Who will go with you?" said Pharaoh to Moses and Aaron.

"We will go with our young and our old, with our sons and our daughters."

"Only the men may go," replied Pharaoh. "Your children must remain here. I refuse to let the entire people go."

Moses and Aaron saw that Egypt would have to be punished further before Pharaoh's heart would be softened.

God commanded Moses to send an eighth plague against Pharaoh. Moses lifted his rod and the sky was darkened with swarms of locusts. The locusts came down on every tree and every green field so that not even a blade of grass remained in Egypt.

The ninth plague was the plague of darkness. For three days and three nights the darkness was so thick that they could not see. People remained rooted in one spot for it was impossible to move about. Only in the land of Goshen, where the children of Israel dwelt, there was light.

Then God said to Moses, "I shall send only one more plague against Egypt. Tell the children of Israel to prepare to leave by midnight tomorrow."

EXERCISES

I. Who said to whom? (Review section 1, pages 145 to 146.)
  1. "From now on do not give them any straw to make bricks."
  2. "What shall we do if they cannot complete the full number of bricks?"
  3. "Do not be lazy. Look and you will find."
  4. "We cannot make bricks without straw."
  5. "Is this how you have freed us from slavery?"

II. Arrange the following sentences in the order in which these things happened. (Review section 2, pages 148 to 149.)
  1. The land of Egypt was covered with frogs.
  2. The children of Israel grew impatient and would not listen.
  3. God said, "Lift your rod and the rivers will turn to blood for seven days."
  4. As soon as the flies disappeared Pharaoh forgot his promise.
  5. "I shall allow your people to leave. But do not go far," said Pharaoh.

III. Answer each question in a complete sentence. (Review section 3, pages 149 to 150.)
  1. What did the dust do to the Egyptians?
  2. What did the hail do to the land?
  3. What did Moses and Aaron reply when Pharaoh offered to let only the men go?
  4. How did the locusts harm Egypt?
  5. What was the ninth plague?

IV. Questions for discussion:
   1. How did Pharaoh show that he deserved to be punished?
   2. Which of these plagues sometimes trouble modern countries? What progress has man made in fighting these plagues?

THINGS TO DO

1. *The Four Questions*—Study the four questions in the *Haggadah* in preparation for the Passover *Seder*.
2. *Passover Songs*—Listen to recordings of Passover songs. Learn to sing them. Some of the favorites are: *Dayenu, Adir Hu, Chad Gadya.*

CHARADES

Choose a Biblical scene such as "The taskmasters and the children of Israel," and act it out in the form of a charade. The team which guesses the title of the scene in the shortest length of time is declared the winner.

CHAPTER XVII

THE HOLIDAY OF PASSOVER

1. THE DEPARTURE FROM EGYPT

MOSES TOLD the children of Israel to be ready to depart from Egypt at midnight. Each family prepared a feast of thanksgiving. They gathered around a lamb and ate quickly, wanderer's staff in hand, ready to leave at any moment.

Then the tenth plague struck. A terrible disease spread throughout Egypt. Pharaoh's first-born son died, and in every home there was sickness and death.

In Goshen, where the children of Israel dwelt, there was no sickness. The angel of death passed over their homes without harming any of the children of Israel. The name Passover is a reminder that sickness and death "passed over" the children of Israel.

Throughout Egypt there was a great cry.

"We will all be dead men soon!" the people said to Pharaoh. "How long will you keep the children of Israel as slaves? Send them away before we are all destroyed."

Pharaoh quickly called for Moses and Aaron.

"Rise up. Go forth from Egypt," he said. "Take with

you your families and all your belongings. Only hurry, before all of us have been slain!"

Large mobs gathered and urged the Israelites to leave quickly. There was no time to lose. The children of Israel left at midnight before they had had an opportunity to bake bread.

They took of their dough which had not yet leavened and baked *matzot* or unleavened bread. They set up their tents in the desert outside of Egypt and thanked God that at last they were free.

And God said to Moses, "Let the children of Israel celebrate the holiday of Passover each year as a reminder that they were freed from slavery in Egypt. For seven days shall they celebrate this holiday of freedom. During that time they must eat *matzot*, or unleavened bread, just as the children of Israel did when they were freed from the house of bondage."

The Hebrew nation has never forgotten these words. For 3500 years we have celebrated the beautiful festival of Passover, and we have thanked God for the precious gift of freedom.

2. AT THE RED SEA

There was a path from Egypt to Canaan along the coast of the sea.

God said to Moses, "Do not take this road even though it is so close to Canaan. If the Philistines attack you, the children of Israel will be frightened and will return to Egypt."

Instead of going by the way of the coast, Moses led the children of Israel through the wilderness toward the Red Sea. Moses carried Joseph's coffin with him for the people had sworn they would bury Joseph in the land of his fathers.

After the Israelites had left, Pharaoh was sorry that he had allowed them to depart.

"What have we done?" said Pharaoh to his servants. "We have allowed Israel to go free. Where can we find such valuable slaves?"

"We can easily bring them back," said one of Pharaoh's captains. "We have received a report that they are lost in the wilderness near the Red Sea."

"Let us overtake them," said Pharaoh. "Get ready the chariots of war. If they try to run away we will chase them into the sea."

The captains of Egypt's army gathered their many chariots and soldiers and followed Israel into the wilderness.

When the children of Israel heard that Pharaoh had pursued after them they became very much frightened.

"Why did you take us to die in the wilderness?" they said to Moses. "Are there no graves in Egypt that we had to come here to die?"

Moses tried to calm them, but the people would not remain silent. "Did we not tell you in Egypt to let us alone that we might serve the Egyptians? It is better to be a slave in Egypt than to die in the wilderness."

And Moses said, "Fear not. God will deliver us today

from the Egyptians so that they will not trouble us again."

All that night a strong wind blew on the waters of the Red Sea. The waters were pushed back to the left and to the right, leaving dry land in the middle.

"Forward," shouted Moses.

At first the children of Israel feared for their lives, but the youths bravely plunged into the sea followed by the entire nation. Soon they reached the other shore.

When morning came Pharaoh saw the children of Israel crossing in the midst of the Red Sea on dry land.

"Quick," shouted Pharaoh to his captains, "let us pursue after them."

The moment the chariots entered the Red Sea their wheels began to sink in the mud. The more they struggled to free themselves the deeper sank their wheels.

Then God said to Moses, "Now you will see the wonders that I will perfom. Wave your rod over the sea and the waters will turn back once more and cover Pharaoh, his chariots and his horsemen."

Moses stretched forth his hand and the waters returned to their usual course. The Egyptians saw the walls of water on their left hand and on their right hand crumbling.

"Flee for your lives," they shouted. It was too late. In a moment the army of Pharaoh and his chariots were covered by the waters of the sea.

Israel had been saved!

Moses and the children of Israel in great joy began to sing a song of praise unto God:

"I will sing unto the Lord, for He is highly exalted

THE SEDER

The horse and his rider hath He thrown into the sea."

Miriam took a timbrel in her hand and led the women in dance. They too sang:

"Sing ye to the Lord, for He is highly exalted
The horse and his rider hath He thrown into the Sea."

3. PASSOVER CELEBRATIONS

Each year we arrange a *Seder* or festive meal to tell the glorious story of Passover, for nothing is more precious to mankind than liberty.

The *Seder* begins with the *Kiddush* or blessing over the cup of wine. Then one of the children seated around the table rises to recite the *Mah Nishtanah* or Four Questions.

"Why is this night different from all other nights? On all other nights we may eat leavened or unleavened bread, but on this night we eat only unleavened bread.

"On all other nights we may eat any kind of herb, but on this night we eat only bitter herbs.

"On all other nights we do not dip our foods at all, but on this night we dip celery into salt-water and the bitter herb into *charoset* (a mixture of almonds, apples, wine and cinnamon.)

"On all other nights we may sit or lean but on this night we all lean."

The father then replies, "All these customs remind us of freedom. Once we were slaves in Egypt but today we are free men."

He then tells the whole story of how the people were freed from slavery, and he explains each custom. "We eat unleavened bread because the children of Israel left Egypt in such haste that they did not have time to allow their bread to leaven. We eat bitter herbs to remind us of the bitter lives that the children of Israel led in Egypt. The celery is a special entrée to show that this is a festive meal. The *charoset* reminds us of the clay that the Israelite slaves made in Egypt. We lean because only free men have the leisure to recline and lean as they eat."

What joy there is at the *Seder* table! At the end of the feast we eat the *afikomen* or dessert consisting of a special piece of *matzah* that has been hidden away.

What fun it is to find the place where the *afikomen* is hidden away! If Father wants the *afikomen* back he'll have to promise us a lovely gift!

Wine, and food, and songs, and games, and presents! Who can ever forget this beautiful holiday of freedom?

4. PASSOVER AND AMERICAN LIBERTY

Although Passover is a Jewish holiday, the whole world knows the story of how Moses freed the slaves and everybody loves this beautiful story.

The American colonists used to read this story and say, "Nothing is more precious to us than our freedom."

In Philadelphia hung a bell on which were written the words of Moses, "Proclaim liberty throughout all the land unto all the inhabitants thereof." When the Declaration of Independence was signed on July 4, 1776 this bell rang out the glad news to the American colonists. This bell, with the words of Moses carved on the outside, is now known as the Liberty Bell.

When Thomas Jefferson and Benjamin Franklin were asked to design a seal for the United States they remembered the story of Israel in Egypt. They proposed as a seal a picture of the children of Israel escaping from Pharaoh. At the bottom were the words, "Rebellion against tyrants is obedience to God." This seal was never officially adopted, but still it shows us how the story of Passover inspired all to fight for freedom.

When the Negro slaves read the Passover story they too thought of freedom. They dreamed of liberty as they sang:

> "Go down, Moses, to Egypt land,
> Tell old Pharaoh,
> Let My people go!"

In every generation the Passover story will inspire people with a love for liberty!

EXERCISES

I. True or false? (Review section 1, pages 153 to 154.)
1. The last plague was the plague of darkness.
2. Pharaoh's first-born son died.
3. The Egyptians told Pharaoh not to let the children of Israel leave Egypt.

OUT OF THE HOUSE OF BONDAGE

4. Passover reminds us that the angel of death "passed over" the homes of the children of Israel without harming them.
5. *Matzah* means "unleavened bread."

II. Complete each sentence. (Review section 2, pages 154 to 158.)

   EGYPT, MIRIAM, PHARAOH, PHILISTINES, RED SEA
   1. If Israel took the short road to Canaan they might have been frightened by war with the _____.
   2. _____ was sorry that he had freed Israel.
   3. The chariots and army of _____ pursued after the children of Israel.
   4. The Israelites crossed on dry land in the midst of the _____.
   5. _____ led the women in singing a song of praise unto God.

III. Match: (Review sections 3 and 4, pages 158 to 160.)

Column A	Column B
Kiddush	1. "Go down Moses to Egypt land."
Four Questions	2. "Proclaim liberty throughout all the land unto all the inhabitants thereof."
Liberty Bell	3. Blessing over the cup of wine.
Franklin and Jefferson	4. "Why is this night different from all other nights?"
Negro spiritual	5. "Rebellion against tyrants is obedience to God."

IV. Questions for discussion:
   1. The slaves did not fully appreciate the value of freedom. What proof can you give that this is true?

2. What did Franklin and Jefferson mean when they said, "Rebellion against tyrants is obedience to God"? What examples can you give of rebellion against tyrants?

THINGS TO DO

1. *Model Seder*—Prepare a model *Seder*. Be sure to include the *Kiddush*, the Four Questions, the answer to the Four Questions, *Dayenu*, the breaking of the *matzah*, the bitter herb and *charoset*, refreshments, the *Afikomen*, *Eleeyahu Ha-Navi*, *Adir Hu*, *Chad Gadya*.
2. *Passover Plate*—Design a Passover plate showing the various objects found on the plate.
3. *Seder Experiences*—Arrange a club period during which each student tells about his impressions of the last *Seder* he visited.

HIDING THE AFIKOMEN—A GAME

The class hides some object which stands for the *afikomen*. The student who is "it" tries to find the *afikomen*. The pupils give him hints by saying "warm" or "hot" when he is near the *afikomen*, and by saying "cold" when he is not close to the *afikomen*. (A variation of this game is to use the piano if there is one in the room. The pianist plays loud music as the student comes near the *afikomen* and soft music when he is not near the *afikomen*.)

UNIT SIX

In the Wilderness

CHAPTER XVIII

AT SINAI

1. BREAD AND WATER

AFTER THEY had crossed over the Red Sea, the children of Israel wandered in the wilderness for several days. The dough they had taken with them from Egypt was now gone, and they had no bread to eat.

The people began to complain bitterly against Moses and Aaron.

"Why did you bring us into the wilderness to kill us all with hunger?" they said. "We wish we had stayed in Egypt. There we sat by the flesh-pots, and we ate bread to the full. Give us bread before we die!"

Moses prayed to God for help.

Then God said to Moses, "I shall rain bread from heaven, and the people will go out and gather their food each day."

The next morning there was a layer of dew near the camp. When the dew dried up the children of Israel found strange food on the ground. The food was fine and scale-like.

The people turned to each other and asked in surprise, "*Man hu?*" ("What is it?")

And Moses replied, "This is the bread which God has given you to eat."

The people gathered in the food and ate it. The food tasted like cake made with honey.

Each morning the people gathered enough food for the day. On Friday, however, they gathered enough food for two days, for no food fell on the Sabbath.

The children of Israel called the food "manna" because they had asked, "*Man hu?*"

When they journeyed on they came to a place where there was no water to drink.

Again they complained bitterly against Moses and Aaron. "Give us water to drink! We are thirsty!"

Moses pleaded with them to be patient, but with no success.

"Why did you bring us up out of Egypt to kill us and our children and our cattle with thirst?" they shouted angrily.

Moses saw that the people were almost ready to stone him. Again he prayed to God for help.

"Go to the rock at the foot of the mountain," God said. "Lift your rod and strike the rock, and water will gush forth."

Moses gathered the children of Israel to the rock and struck it with his rod. Suddenly water spouted forth! Moses had uncovered a secret spring.

The children of Israel drank the water of the fountain, and they stopped their complaints against Moses and Aaron.

2. WAR WITH AMALEK

When the people of Amalek saw how weak the children of Israel were because of their wanderings they said, "Let us attack Israel for we can easily defeat them!"

Scouts came running to Moses, "An army is approaching. Amalek has come to war against Israel."

Moses chose Joshua to head the army of Israel. Joshua gathered the young men of Israel and prepared them for the battle.

The next morning when Amalek attacked, Moses went up to the top of the hill to watch the battle. With Moses were his brother, Aaron, and his nephew, Hur, the son of Miriam.

Moses raised his rod and prayed to God for victory. And it came to pass that when Moses held up his hands, Israel began to win; but when Moses was tired and he let down his hands, Amalek began to win. Aaron stood at one side and held up one hand, and Hur stood at the other side and held up the other hand.

When the sun went down and evening came, Moses saw that Joshua had won a glorious victory. Amalek fled in fear and Israel gave thanks to God for their victory in battle.

The people of Israel swore that they would never forget Amalek's cowardly act. Amalek remained one of Israel's chief enemies for many years, and was later punished by Israel's first king.

3. THE TEN COMMANDMENTS

Led by a pillar of cloud by day and a pillar of fire by night, the children of Israel continued their wanderings until they came to the wilderness of Sinai.

And God said to Moses, "The time has come for the children of Israel to renew the covenant that I made with Abraham, Isaac and Jacob. Let the people listen to My laws and I shall bless them and make them a holy nation."

When Moses repeated these words to the children of Israel, they said, "All that God has spoken we will do."

And the Lord said unto Moses, "Go unto the people and tell them to wash their garments. Let them be ready for the third day when I shall appear unto them on Mount Sinai."

On the third day the people gathered at the foot of Mount Sinai. A thick cloud covered the mountain. There were loud peals of thunder and bright flashes of lighting. In the distance could be heard the sound of the *shofar*.

Suddenly from the mountain a voice proclaimed the ten commandments:

1. I am the Lord thy God, who brought thee out of the land of Egypt, out of the house of bondage.
2. Thou shalt have no other gods before Me.
3. Thou shalt not take the name of the Lord thy God in vain.
4. Remember the Sabbath day, to keep it holy.
5. Honor thy father and thy mother.
6. Thou shalt not kill.

MOSES AND THE TEN COMMANDMENTS

7. Thou shalt not commit adultery.
8. Thou shalt not steal.
9. Thou shalt not bear false witness against thy neighbor.
10. Thou shalt not covet.

The children of Israel heard the ten commandments and said, "We will do as the Lord requires and we will obey."

4. THE IMPORTANCE OF THE TEN COMMANDMENTS

The ten commandments are Israel's greatest gift to mankind. We are told that God gave the ten commandments in the desert so that no one nation would say, "These commandments were given in my land only." The ten commandments were meant for the whole world.

There are many reasons why the other religions accepted the ten commandments from Judaism, the mother religion.

a) The ten commandments teach us to believe in one God and not to worship idols.

b) The ten commandments teach us the importance of family love. The fifth commandment tells us to honor our parents, and the seventh commandment warns husband and wife to be true to each other.

c) The ten commandments teach us to rest on the Sabbath. The Hebrew nation was the first nation to observe a rest day once a week. Now every country has accepted the idea of a Sabbath and sets aside a day when people can rest from their work.

d) The ten commandments teach us to do what is right.

IN THE WILDERNESS

The third commandment teaches us not to swear falsely. We are told not to kill or steal. The ninth commandment tells us not to lie about others, and the last commandment warns us not to want what belongs to others.

In honor of the giving of the ten commandments we celebrate the holiday of Shavuot. It was at this season too that first fruits were later brought to the Temple that was built in Jerusalem.

Shavuot, or the Feast of Weeks, is so called because seven weeks passed between the departure from Egypt and the giving of the ten commandments and the Torah (Law).

Today we decorate the synagogue with green leaves on Shavuot. We read the ten commandments, and honor the students who have finished a course of study in the Torah.

EXERCISES

I. Answer each question in a full sentence. (Review section 1, pages 165 to 167.)
   1. Why did Israel complain after the crossing of the Red Sea?
   2. How much food did the people gather on Friday?
   3. Why was the food called "manna"?
   4. Why did the children of Israel complain again?
   5. How did Moses get water for the people?

II. Amalek or Israel? (Review section 2, page 167.)
   1. _____ started the war.
   2. _____ was weak because of its wanderings in the desert.

3. Joshua was captain of _____.
4. When Moses lifted his hands _____ won.
5. Joshua won a glorious victory over _____.

III. Fill in the correct number. (Review sections 3 and 4, pages 168 to 171.)
1. The children of Israel received _____ commandments at Sinai.
2. The _____ commandment says, "Honor thy father and thy mother."
3. The _____ commandment says, "Thou shalt not kill."
4. The _____ commandment says, "Thou shalt not steal."
5. Shavuot comes _____ weeks after Passover.

IV. Questions for discussion:
1. Why are the ten commandments so important?
2. How is *Shavuot* observed in your synagogue?

THINGS TO DO

1. *Memory Gem*—Memorize the ten commandments.
2. *Research*—Dairy foods such as blintzes are popular on *Shavuot* since the Torah is compared to "honey and milk." Mention some favorite foods for the following holidays:
Rosh Ha-Shanah, Chanukah, Tu Bishvat, Purim, Passover.
3. *The Ten Commandments*—Draw a cover for your scrapbook or class magazine using the ten commandments as a cover design.

A PUZZLE

Write the name of the city in which Jacob met Rachel. Add the second letter of the fifth commandment. Subtract the letters in the name of the brother of Moses. Add the city in which Abraham was born.

The answer is the name of a person mentioned in this chapter.

CHAPTER XIX

AFTER SINAI

1. THE GOLDEN CALF

MOSES CLIMBED to the top of Mount Sinai to receive the tablets of stone on which were written the ten commandments, and to learn the other laws of the Torah.

Moses remained on the top of Mount Sinai for many days. When the children of Israel saw that Moses did not return they grew very impatient.

"Where is Moses who brought us out of Egypt?" they asked.

Aaron tried to calm the people by telling them how long it took to write down the words of the Torah. But the people did not believe him.

At last the children of Israel came to Aaron in great anger, and said, "Up! Make us a god who shall go before us! We don't know what has happened to Moses who took us out of Egypt, and we must have a god to help us."

Aaron was greatly puzzled. He knew that Moses would return after the fortieth day on Mount Sinai. The people were so impatient that they might stone their leaders before Moses returned.

Aaron thought, "Perhaps I can delay them without denying their request."

He turned to the people and said, "Bring me your earrings, and your jewelry, and your gold and silver."

Aaron thought that it would take a long time to gather the jewelry together. By that time Moses would return.

To Aaron's great surprise the people were so anxious to have a new god that they quickly brought their earrings and their jewelry.

Many Egyptians had joined with the children of Israel when they left Egypt. Several Egyptians who were artists now stepped forward. They lighted a great fire and melted down the jewelry. They now began to form a large golden calf.

In Egypt the children of Israel had often seen the Egyptians worship calves and bulls. Although they had promised at Sinai not to worship idols, it was easy for them to imitate the Egyptians in whose midst they had lived for so many years.

The people now began to shout with joy and to say, "This is your god, O Israel, which freed you from slavery in Egypt."

The next day they made a great feast unto the golden calf. They brought sacrifices to the calf. Then they ate and drank and danced merrily around the calf.

2. THE BROKEN TABLETS

When the children of Israel danced around the golden calf, God urged Moses to return to the foot of the mountain.

"Go down quickly to the camp, for Israel has begun to worship an idol. They have made a golden calf, and have declared that this is their god."

Moses sadly prepared to leave Mount Sinai. He prayed to God to forgive the great sin of Israel.

"I shall destroy Israel and make of your children a great nation," said God to Moses.

"Remember Your promise to Abraham, Isaac and Jacob," said Moses. "I do not care for any reward for myself or my family, but I pray that You will pardon Israel."

"I have heard your prayer," replied God, "and will forgive them."

Moses quickly climbed down to the foot of the mountain where Joshua was waiting for him.

"I hear the sound of war in the camp," said Joshua anxiously when he saw Moses.

"This is not the sound of war," said Moses. "You hear singing and rejoicing."

Moses and Joshua walked toward the camp. In his hands Moses carried the precious tablets of stone on which were inscribed the ten commandments.

When Moses came near the camp and saw the people dancing, he could not control his anger.

"You have sinned greatly against the Lord!" said Moses to the people.

Lifting his hands in anger, Moses threw the two tablets of stone to the earth and shattered the tablets into many pieces.

Moses then burnt the golden calf with fire until nothing remained but ashes and powder. Moses punished the leaders who had urged the people to worship an idol. The people prayed that God would pardon their sin.

Moses then returned to Mount Sinai to receive a new set of tablets. Again he remained for forty days and forty nights. When Moses returned a special ark was built in which the tablets of stone were placed. And the children of Israel carried with them the ark of God wherever they went.

3. THE TORAH

Moses now taught the people the many laws of the Torah.

He taught the people to be kind, and truthful and good. "Love your neighbor as yourself," said Moses. The Rabbis later said that this was the golden rule of brotherhood on which the whole Torah was based.

"Be kind to strangers," taught Moses, "because you were strangers in the land of Egypt."

"Justice, justice shalt thou pursue," said Moses to the people. He taught them not to take bribes and to be honest in all their dealings. He warned them against using false weights and measures.

Hebrews were not allowed to be slaves. A Hebrew worker might hire himself out for six years, but in the seventh year he must go free.

Moses warned the people to take good care of the poor, the orphans and the widows. Every farmer had to leave the corners of the field to the poor. When a farmer cut his grain in the field, he had to leave for the poor whatever grain fell to the ground.

Every seventh day was a rest day or Sabbath. In the same manner every seventh year was a rest year for the soil. The farmer had to let the land rest for a year so that it would regain its strength and fertility.

These were some of the many wise laws in the Torah that Moses taught to the children of Israel.

EXERCISES

I. True or false? (Review section 1, pages 174 to 175.)
1. Moses and Aaron stayed at the top of Mount Sinai.
2. The people wanted Aaron to make an idol.
3. Aaron tried to delay the making of the idol.
4. The children of Israel had seen the Egyptians worship idols.
5. The children of Israel sacrificed to the sun and moon.

II. Who said to whom? (Review section 2, pages 176 to 177.)
1. "Remember Your promise to Abraham, Isaac and Jacob."
2. "I have heard your prayer."
3. "I hear the sound of war in the camp."

IN THE WILDERNESS

    4. "This is not the sound of war. You hear singing and rejoicing."
    5. "You have sinned greatly against the Lord."

III. Mention 5 things in the Torah that Moses taught to the children of Israel. (Review section 3, pages 177 to 178.)

IV. Questions for discussion:
    1. Mention examples of people who have lived up to the rule, "Love your neighbor as yourself." Can you think of any examples of people who have not lived up to this rule?
    2. Moses taught the people to be kind to strangers. Are we kind to foreigners today?

THINGS TO DO

1. *The Two Tablets*—Make a replica of the two tablets using clay, or copper, or soap, or wood.

2. *A Sabbath Project*—Prepare a Sabbath table including the candles, the *Kiddush* cup and the *chalah* (bread for the Sabbath). One student may recite the blessing over the candles; another student may recite the blessings for wine and bread. Sing some Sabbath songs.

THREE-MINUTE QUIZ

Write down the names of as many people mentioned in this book as you can think of. The time limit is three minutes. The student who lists the greatest number of names is the winner.

CHAPTER XX

REBELLION

1. THE TWELVE SPIES

THE CHILDREN of Israel were now ready to enter the land of Canaan.

Moses picked twelve men, one from each tribe to serve as scouts.

"See what the land is like," said Moses. "And see what the people who dwell in the land are like, whether they are strong or weak. Find out whether they live in strong cities or in open camps. And bring back examples of the fruits of the land."

The spies then went to Canaan where they spent forty days. They brought back figs and pomegranates and other fruits. They also cut down a large branch with a cluster of grapes. So large was the branch that two people had to carry the grapes.

When the spies returned they said, "We came into the land of Canaan, and this is the fruit of it. Indeed it is a land flowing with milk and with honey. But the people who live in the land are fierce, and their cities are strong."

Two of the spies, Joshua and Caleb, stepped forward and

IN THE WILDERNESS

THE FRUITS OF CANAAN

said, "We should go up at once and enter the land. We are well able to conquer it."

"We are not able to go up," said the other ten spies. "The men we saw are giants, and we are in their eyes like grasshoppers. We shall never be able to conquer the land!"

When the people heard the report of the ten spies they began to weep. "If only we had died in the land of Egypt!" they said. "It would even have been better to die in the wilderness than to die by the sword. Should we not try to return to Egypt?"

Moses and Aaron begged the people not to complain. "Have you not heard the report of Joshua and Caleb?" asked Moses. "Do not rebel against God. He will help us to enter the land which He has promised to Abraham, Isaac and Jacob."

The tribe of Levi, to which Moses and Aaron belonged, wanted to obey the words of Moses. The other Israelites, however, would not listen.

"Let us pick a captain who will bring us back to Egypt." they shouted.

God became very angry when the people complained.

"They still have the hearts of slaves and are not brave enough to enter the land of Canaan. As a punishment they will wander in the desert for forty years until all the adults have died. Then their children, who have the hearts of free men, will enter the land. Of the older generation only Joshua and Caleb and the tribe of Levi will see the promised land."

When Moses told the people of their punishment they

wept. But it was too late. Some men tried to form an army to conquer Canaan. Moses warned them they would not succeed. Indeed they were cut down in battle as soon as they met the first unfriendly tribe.

Instead of entering Canaan the Israelites continued to wander in the desert.

2. THE WATERS OF MERIBAH

Again and again the people rebelled. Once they complained because they had become tired of the manna. At another time those who were jealous of Aaron complained because he had been appointed *Kohen Gadol* or High Priest.

Once the people challenged Moses saying, "Who made you our leader?" Always Moses was calm and patient, and tried to teach the people to have faith in God.

After many years the people came to a place in the desert called Kadesh. But there was no water in Kadesh, and the people began to complain bitterly.

"Why did you bring us out of Egypt to this desert? There is no water here, and we and our children and cattle will die of thirst."

Moses prayed to God for help.

And God said, "Now the people will see the miracle that I will perform. Gather the people and speak unto the rock that it may give forth water."

Moses gathered the people and said, "Hear now, you rebels. Out of this rock will I bring forth water."

Moses remembered how once before he had struck the rock and water had gushed forth from a secret fountain.

And Moses thought to himself, "Surely God wants me again to strike the rock."

Moses lifted his rod and hit the rock twice. Water came forth and the people drank.

God was angry at Moses, however, because he had not obeyed His words exactly. By striking the rock instead of speaking to it, Moses had failed to show the miracle which God wanted to perform.

"You did not obey My words," said God. "Because you did not show faith in me, you will not lead the people into Canaan."

This was the greatest disappointment in the life of Moses. But Moses knew he should not have lost his temper or disobeyed God's exact words.

He also knew that his work would be finished after he had led the people through the wilderness to the gates of Canaan.

The fountain which Moses had brought forth was called "Meribah" which means "argument" or "strife," because of the argument over the water.

3. IN THE DESERT—SUKKOT

The children of Israel wandered from place to place for forty years.

They built a tabernacle or great tent in which they worshiped God. In the tabernacle stood a large candlestick of gold with seven branches, and the ark containing the ten commandments.

Aaron and his sons were the *Kohanim*, or priests, who were in charge of the tabernacle.

Wherever the Israelites went they carried the tabernacle with them. The camp was always built around the tabernacle with three tribes on each side.

Often the people would enter the tabernacle to thank God for all the wonders He had performed. They had been freed from slavery; they had been saved from the waters of the Red Sea; they had been delivered from hostile tribes, from hunger and from thirst.

Today we celebrate the holiday of *Sukkot* to remind us of the wandering of the children of Israel in the desert. A *Sukkah* is a booth, or hut, thatched with leaves and grass. The Israelites often built such huts in the desert in which to live.

What a delight it is to enter the *Sukkah!* The hut is decorated with grapes and apples and other fruits. As we enter we recite the blessing over wine as a sign of joy that we have received so many blessings from God.

Later in Israel the farmers also celebrated *Sukkot* because it was the time of the grape harvest. Many a farmer would sleep in the *Sukkah*, or booth, in the field during the harvest season.

Moses commanded the children of Israel never to forget their special holidays.

Passover, the spring holiday coming at the time of the barley harvest, reminded the people that God had freed them from slavery in Egypt. *Shavuot,* the summer holiday coming at the time of the wheat harvest and first fruits, reminded the people that God had given them the ten commandments at Sinai. *Sukkot,* the autumn holiday coming at the time of the grape harvest, reminded the people that God had led the Israelites safely through the wilderness for forty years.

Sukkot served as the model for a beautiful American holiday—the festival of Thanksgiving. The Pilgrim Fathers who read the Bible every day of their lives felt that they were like the children of Israel.

They too had left the old country looking for freedom and for a chance to worship God as they believed. They too had faced many dangers in the wilderness. They too had been delivered from danger and had received the blessing of God.

The Pilgrim Fathers said, "When the children of Israel were led by God through the wilderness they offered thanks to Him for His many blessings. We too will celebrate a holiday of thanksgiving unto God."

EXERCISES

I. Why? (Review section 1, pages 180 to 183.)
   1. Why did Moses send twelve spies to Canaan?
   2. Why did the spies bring back fruit from Canaan?
   3. Why did the spies say, "We are not able to go up to Canaan"?

IN THE WILDERNESS

    4. Why did God make the Israelites wander in the desert for forty years?
    5. Why were Joshua and Caleb and the tribe of Levi not punished?

II. Match: (Review section 2, pages 183 to 184.)

Column A   *Column B*
Aaron   1. waters of argument
Kadesh   2. *Kohen Gadol* (high priest)
manna   3. place in the desert
Meribah   4. struck the rock
Moses   5. desert food

III. Name the holiday. (Review section 3, pages 184 to 186.)
    1. _____ reminds us that the children of Israel were freed from slavery in Egypt.
    2. _____ reminds us of the granting of the ten commandments at Sinai.
    3. _____ reminds us of the wandering of the children of Israel in the desert.
    4. _____ reminds us of the wheat harvest and of the first fruits of the land.
    5. _____ reminds us of the American holiday of Thanksgiving.

IV. Questions for discussion:
    1. How did the children of Israel show that they were still slaves in spirit?
    2. How did the Bible influence American history?

THINGS TO DO

    1. *Model Sukkah*—Build a miniature *Sukkah* of boards and leaves. Decorate it with fruits.

2. *Picture Calendar*—Make a calendar using a holiday design for each month. Here are some suggestions based on the month in which each holiday usually falls:

September—Rosh Ha-Shanah
October—Yom Kippur; or Sukkot
November—Thanksgiving
December—Chanukah
January—Tu Bishvat (Israel Arbor Day)
February—Lincoln's or Washington's Birthday
March—Purim
April—Passover
May—Lag B'Omer; or Israel Independence Day
June—Shavuot
July—The 4th of July
August—Tisha B'Av (the day on which the Temple fell)

NUMBER PUZZLE

Write the number of tribes of Israel. Divide by the number of Isaac's sons. Add the number of commandments heard at Sinai. Add the number of Joseph's brothers. Subtract the number of Jochebed's children. Add the number of days in the week on which the manna fell. Add the number of years that the children of Israel wandered in the desert.

The answer will equal the number of the elders of Israel picked by Moses to help him judge the children of Israel.

CHAPTER XXI

NEAR THE LAND OF CANAAN

1. EAST OF THE JORDAN

MOSES HAD LED the people through the desert for forty years. He now had to make plans to cross the Jordan River into Canaan.

Between the children of Israel and Canaan lay the land belonging to Edom, the nation descended from Esau.

Moses sent messengers to Edom saying, "You know how God has saved us from slavery in Egypt. Now help your brother, Israel, by letting us pass through your land to Canaan. We will not turn aside unto your fields or vineyards. If we drink water we will pay for whatever we drink."

Edom replied, "You shall not pass through. If you try, we will come up against you with the sword."

Moses did not want to war against the people of Edom since they were related to the children of Israel. Instead he turned north and sent the same message to Sihon, king of Heshbon.

"Allow us to pass through your land. We promise we will touch nothing belonging to you."

Sihon's answer was—battle! He gathered a large army and attacked the children of Israel. But Joshua fought bravely at the head of the army of Israel and defeated Sihon.

Og, a giant who was king of Bashan, now attacked the camp of Israel. He too was defeated and his cities were conquered.

The children of Israel now owned a large stretch of land east of the Jordan River. They were ready to cross and to enter the promised land.

The leaders of the tribes of Reuben, Gad and half of Manasseh then came to Moses with a special request.

"The land we have conquered is excellent for cattle. We have much cattle. Allow us to settle in this section of land east of the Jordan."

Moses at first was very angry. "Do you expect your brothers to cross the Jordan and to face many dangers while you remain in safety in your homes?"

"We will go with our brothers," they replied. "But we will build homes for our wives and children here. When the other tribes have received their share of the land then we will return to our homes east of the Jordan."

"If you go up armed and help your brothers, then indeed you may have this section as your inheritance," said Moses.

The tribes of Reuben, Gad and Manasseh thanked Moses. Then they began to build cities for their families while they prepared to march forward with the other tribes across the Jordan.

2. BALAK AND BALAAM

When Balak, the king of Moab, saw what had happened to Sihon and Og he became greatly frightened.

"I am afraid of the children of Israel," said the king to his advisers. "If they enter Moab they will destroy whatever we have, the way an ox eats up every blade of grass in the field. What shall we do?"

"We need the help of Balaam, the wise man," said one of the advisers. "If he pronounces a curse on the children of Israel they will be unable to harm us."

The king sent to Balaam saying, "Behold, there is a people called Israel that has just come out from Egypt. They are too mighty for me. But if you curse them, perhaps I shall be able to drive them away."

At first Balaam refused, but the king of Moab sent another group of messengers.

"Let nothing prevent you from coming. I will honor you greatly if you come, and reward you with gold and silver."

Balaam could not resist this offer. The next day he saddled his donkey and journeyed to Moab with the messengers.

Suddenly the donkey moved off the road into a field. Balaam began to beat the donkey until it returned to a narrow path between two vineyards.

The donkey pressed against the fence crushing poor Balaam's foot.

"Look out for my foot!" shouted Balaam to the donkey kicking it without mercy.

The donkey walked on for a few steps, then lay down without moving.

"Move on!" shouted Balaam. "Move on!"

The donkey would not budge. Balaam picked up a stick and beat the donkey again and again.

The donkey was in such pain that it began to make fearful sounds. To Balaam's great surprise it seemed as if the donkey spoke in human language.

"Why do you beat me?" the donkey seemed to say. "What did I do that was wrong? Am I not your beloved donkey on whom you have been riding all of your life?"

"You're too stubborn," shouted Balaam. "If I had a sword in my hand I would kill you!"

Just then Balaam looked up and saw an angel with a sword in his hand standing in his path.

"Your donkey saved your life three times," said the angel, "for I was ready to slay you. Why are you going to curse Israel? Do you not know that Israel has been blessed by God?"

"I have sinned," said Balaam. "I shall return to my home, if you wish."

"Go with the men," said the angel. "But speak only the words that I shall put into your mouth."

3. THE BLESSING

When Balaam came to Moab, the king brought him to a mountain top from which he could see the camp of Israel.

"Build seven altars," said Balaam, "and sacrifice a sheep on each altar. Then I shall tell you the word of God."

When the sacrifices had been made, Balaam looked out at the camp of Israel and said:

> "How can I curse whom the Lord has blessed?
> Praised among nations be Israel!"

When Balak heard Balaam's words of praise he became very angry.

"Is this the way you curse Israel?" he asked.

"I told you I can only say what the Lord puts into my mouth," answered Balaam.

"Come to another place," said Balak. "Maybe you will be able to curse Israel from this place."

They climbed another mountain. Balak again set up seven altars and sacrificed seven sheep.

Balaam looked out at the camp of Israel and said:

> "The Lord has ordered me to bless
> Can I disobey the Lord's command?
> For the tribes of Jacob shall be like a star."

"Don't bless and don't curse," pleaded Balak. "That is enough."

But Balaam continued his blessing. As he saw the twelve tribes of Israel spread out before him at the foot of the mountain, he noticed the orderly arrangement around the tabernacle. How peaceful everything seemed to be!

Once more Balaam began to bless the children of Israel:

> "How beautiful are thy tents, O Jacob,
> Your dwelling-places, O Israel."

The king of Moab saw that Israel was indeed blessed, and he returned to his city.

Moses warned the children of Israel not to war against Moab even though the king was so unfriendly because Moab was descended from Lot, the nephew of Abraham.

Balaam's words in praise of Israel were so beautiful that we sing them to this very day as we enter the synagogue.

EXERCISES

I. What is my name? (Review section 1, pages 189 to 190.)
1. I am the ancestor of the twelve tribes. Sometimes I am called Israel, but I also have another name.
2. I am the ancestor of Edom. My descendants refused to allow Israel to pass through their land.
3. I was king of Heshbon. I refused to allow Israel to enter my borders.
4. I was King of Bashan. Even though I was a giant I was defeated by Israel.
5. I was leader of Israel. I gave 2½ tribes permission to settle east of the Jordan.

II. Who said to whom? (Review section 2, pages 191 to 192.)
1. "I am afraid of the children of Israel."
2. "If you curse them, perhaps I shall be able to drive them away."
3. "If I had a sword in my hand I would kill you!"
4. "I have sinned. I shall return to my home, if you wish."
5. "Speak only the words that I shall put into your mouth."

III. True or false? (Review section 3, pages 192 to 194.)
   1. Balak was king of Edom.
   2. Balak wanted Balaam to curse Israel.
   3. Balaam blessed Israel many times.
   4. Moab and Israel went to war with each other.
   5. Balaam's blessing was so beautiful we still recite his words as we enter the synagogue.

IV. Questions for discussion:
   1. Compare Moses and Lincoln.
   2. Is the attitude of the Arab nations toward Israel today the same as the attitude of Edom and Moab?

THINGS TO DO

1. *Balaam's Blessing*—The blessing recited by Balaam begins with the words "*Mah Tovu*". Learn to sing this song.

2. *Home-Made Movies*—The class can make its own movies by drawing pictures of Israel in Egypt and in the wilderness. Attach the pictures, pasted together, to two rollers. Unroll one picture at a time.

3. *Show and Tell*—Each student displays and explains the projects he has finished this term. Invite parents or another class.

SCRAMBLED NAMES—A PUZZLE

Unscramble the following names. When properly arranged the letters will spell out the names of people well known in Jewish history.

1. SESOM
2. AAABLM
3. HONIS
4. RAANO
5. USAHOJ
6. AAICS
7. IAMIRM
8. AAABHMR
9. HEPSOJ
10. ABCJO

CHAPTER XXII

THE LAST DAYS OF MOSES

1. THE DEATH OF AARON

MIRIAM, the sister of Moses, passed away while the people camped near Kadesh. For forty years this great woman had helped the women of Israel to understand the need for freedom.

As the children of Israel marched northward toward Canaan, they passed Mount Hor, near the land of Edom.

Then God said to Moses, "Aaron shall be gathered unto his fathers. He shall not enter the promised land."

And Moses asked, "Who will serve in the tabernacle in his place?"

And God replied, "Eleazar his son will be *Kohen Gadol* in place of Aaron."

Moses, Aaron and Eleazar then climbed Mount Hor. Aaron was dressed in his beautiful priestly garments.

Moses stripped Aaron of his garments and put them on his son, Eleazar. This was a sign that Eleazar would be the new *Kohen Gadol*.

Aaron then died peacefully at the top of Mount Hor.

Aaron was one of the great leaders of Israel:

a) As spokesman for Israel he helped free the slaves from Egyptian bondage.

b) He taught the children of Israel patience whenever danger faced them in the desert. Even when Aaron told the people to bring their jewelry for the golden calf, his real purpose was to delay until Moses returned.

c) As first *Kohen Gadol*, or High Priest, Aaron taught the children of Israel to worship God with pure hearts.

2. "HEAR, O ISRAEL..."

After their battles with Sihon and Og, the children of Israel rested near the Jordan River. Across the river, the beautiful palm trees of Jericho swayed in the wind. Behind them was the desert in which they had wandered for forty years.

Moses said to the people, "Gather together, and I shall give you my final message before I die."

The children of Israel assembled to hear the last words of their great leader.

Moses pointed across the river toward Jericho.

"The promised land lies before you," said Moses. "But God will give you this land only if you carry out His laws of truth and justice."

Moses reminded the people of their mistakes. He mentioned the making of the golden calf, and the cowardly report brought back from Canaan by the ten spies. He warned them never to worship idols or to disobey God.

Moses lifted his voice, looking directly at the people, as he said in Hebrew:

"Shma Yisrael Adonai Elohenu Adonai Echad."

("Hear, O Israel, the Lord is Our God, the Lord is One.")

Then Moses continued:

"And thou shalt love the Lord thy God with all thy heart, and with all thy soul, and with all thy might. And these words which I command thee this day, shall be upon thy heart. And thou shalt teach them diligently unto thy children, and shalt talk of them when thou sittest in thy house, and when thou walkest by the way, and when thou liest down and when thou risest up. And thou shalt bind them for a sign upon thy hand, and they shall be for frontlets between thine eyes. And thou shalt write them upon the door-posts of thy house, and upon thy gates."

We repeat these words each day in our prayers because they teach us so many fine lessons:

a) We must love God.

b) We must always keep in our hearts God's command to be kind and good.

c) We must teach these laws of kindness and truth to our children.

d) We must carry out the ceremonies of our religion which remind us of these laws.

One such ceremony is attaching the *mezuzah* to our door-posts, as we were commanded by Moses. The *mezuzah* is a copper case containing the words of the *Shma Yisrael*.

When we see the *mezuzah* we think of the *Shma Yisrael* and we say to ourselves, "All who enter here are reminded to love God and to carry out His commands of truth and kindness."

3. THE DEATH OF MOSES

Moses wrote down all the laws that he had taught unto the children of Israel.

He called Eleazar, the son of Aaron, and said, "Keep this book and teach it to the children of Israel. That will be the duty of all the members of the tribe of Levi."

Moses then called Joshua and appointed him to be the new leader of Israel.

"Be strong and of good courage," said Moses. "You will lead the children of Israel into the land which the Lord swore unto our fathers. God will be with you if only the people obey His laws."

Moses and Joshua entered the tabernacle together and prayed to God that He would help Joshua to lead the people into Canaan.

A pillar of cloud appeared in the tabernacle. The people saw and knew that God had appointed Joshua to be the successor of Moses.

Then God said to Moses, "Climb to the top of Mount Nebo. From there you will be able to see the promised land. After that you will be gathered unto your fathers."

Moses said farewell to Joshua and to the children of Israel.

The people looked up at their great leader with tears in their eyes. Moses was now 120 years old, yet he was still strong and vigorous. He had taken them out of the land of slavery. He had taught them the ten commandments and the laws of the Torah. For forty years he had faced all the dangers of the wilderness with wisdom and courage. His love for Israel had never failed even in the darkest moments.

Moses climbed to the top of Mount Nebo. He looked out toward the promised land.

"This is indeed a land flowing with milk and with honey," thought Moses.

He saw the palm-trees of Jericho, the waters of the Jordan and the Dead Sea, the hills around Jerusalem, the rich soil of the plains and the valleys.

"Even though I cannot enter, I have seen the promised land with my own eyes. Soon the children of Israel will possess the land that God has sworn to Abraham, Isaac and Jacob. My work is done!"

Moses died and was buried east of the Jordan River.

The people mourned many days for Moses, the great leader who had given them freedom and who had taught them to love the Torah.

EXERCISES

I. Choose the correct name or phrase. (Review section 1, pages 197 to 198.)
  1. The women of Israel were led in the desert by _____. (Miriam, Sarah)

2. Aaron died near _____. (Egypt, Edom)
3. Eleazar was Aaron's _____. (nephew, son)
4. Eleazar became the new _____. (captain, high priest)
5. The first *Kohen Gadol* was _____. (Aaron, Moses)

II. Mention 4 reasons why the *Shma Yisrael* is so important. (Review section 2, pages 198 to 200.)

III. Complete each sentence. (Review section 3, pages 200 to 201.)
1. Moses gave a copy of the laws to _____.
2. Teaching the Torah was the duty of the tribe of _____.
3. The new leader of Israel was _____.
4. God told Moses to climb to the top of Mount _____.
5. From the mountain top, Moses saw the entire land of _____.

IV. Questions for discussion:
1. How did Miriam and Aaron help the people of Israel?
2. How did Joshua prove he deserved to be the new leader?

REVIEW QUESTIONS

for Units Five and Six (pages 129 to 202)

1. Why is Moses called the greatest leader in Jewish history?
2. Which is the most exciting chapter in Units Five and Six? Why?

IN THE WILDERNESS

3. What do the holidays Passover, Shavuot and Sukkot teach us about Jewish history?
4. Write a sentence about each of any ten of the following: Jochebed, Miriam, Midian, Jethro, Zipporah, Aaron, Pharaoh, Red Sea, *afikomen*, Sinai, Amalek, Hur, Joshua, Caleb, Meribah, Edom, Sihon, Og, Moab, Balak, Balaam, Eleazar, *mezuzah*.

TEST

on Units Five and Six

I. Who am I? (30 points)
   1. I was the first *Kohen Gadol*. I helped Moses free the Israelites from slavery.
   2. I was one of the 12 spies. Joshua and I gave a good report about Canaan.
   3. I lived in Midian. Moses was my son-in-law.
   4. I watched Moses when his mother hid him in the bulrushes. I led the women of Israel in song when we crossed the Red Sea.
   5. I was ordered to curse the children of Israel, but instead I blessed them.
   6. I was picked as leader of Israel to succeed Moses.

II. Why? (30 points)
   1. Why do we celebrate Passover?
   2. Why do we eat *matzah* on Passover?
   3. Why do we celebrate *Shavuot?*
   4. Why do we celebrate *Sukkot?*
   5. Why do we attach a *mezuzah* to the door-posts of our houses?

III. Choose the correct word or phrase. (20 points)
1. The first plague was the plague of (blood, frogs, darkness).
2. When Israel came out of Egypt it was attacked by (Amalek, Edom, Moab).
3. The Pilgrim Fathers modeled the holiday of Thanksgiving after (Passover, Shavuot, Sukkot).
4. The children of Israel danced around the golden calf when (Moses struck the rock, Moses said they would wander in the desert for forty years, Moses delayed in coming down from Mount Sinai).
5. The ten spies did not want to enter Canaan because (they thought the Egyptians would pursue them, the land was not fertile, they were afraid of the people of Canaan).

IV. Answer (a) or (b). (20)
(a) Mention 4 reasons why Moses is called the greatest leader in Jewish history.
(b) Mention 4 reasons why *Shma Yisrael* is an important prayer.

Guide to Pronunciation

KEY

ärm	thēre	nŏt
hăt	thêy	môre
câre	înk	rūle
āte	īce	ŭp
ēat	ïll	fûr
ĕnd	ōld	ṡ as in "waṡ"

Glossary

Aâr′on
Ā′bra-ham
Ā′bram
Ăd′am
Ä-dir′hu
ä-fi-kô′men
Ăm′a-lĕk
ăm′ram
Ăsh′er

Bā′bel ("a" as in "ate")
Băb′y-lon
Bā′laam (first "a" as in "ate")
Bā′lak ("a" as in "ate")

Bā′shan
Bē′er-shē′ba
Bĕn′ja-mĭn
Bĕth′El
Bĕth′-le-hem
Be-thū′el
brĭth

Cāin
Cā′leb
Cā′naan (first "a" as in "ate")
Chäd Gäd-ya′ (guttural "ch")
Chä-nu-kah′ (guttural "ch")
cha-rô′set (guttural "ch")

205

GLOSSARY

cov′e-nant ("o" as in "cover")
cov′et ("o" as in "cover")

Da-măs′cŭs
Dăn
Dä-yê′nu
Dī′nah

Ē′dom
Ē′lam
Ele-ā′zar
Ê-lee-yä′hu Hä-Nä-vî′
Eli-ē′zer ("e" as in "eat")
Ē′phra-ĭm ("e" as in "eat")
Ē′phron
Ē′sau
Eu-phrā′tes

Găd
Gĭl′e-ad
Go-mŏr′rah
Gō′shen

Hā′gar
Hag-ga-dah′
Hā′ran
Hē′bron ("e" as in "eat")
Hĕsh′bŏn
Hôr
Hûr (rhymes with "fur")

Ī′saac
Ĭsh′ma-el
Ĭs′ra-el (3 syllables)

Ĭs′sa-char ("ch" as in "Jericho")

Jā′cob
Jĕr′i-chō
Je-ru′sa-lem
Jē′thrō ("e" as in "eat")
Jôr′dan
Jŏch′e-bĕd ("ch" as in "Jericho")
Jō′seph ("s" as in "was")
Jŏsh′u-a
Jū′dah

Kā′desh
Kid-dūsh′
Kô-hän-im′
Kô-hĕn′ Gä-dôl′

Lā′ban
Läg B′Ô′mer
Lē′ah
Lē′vī ("i" as in "ice")
Lŏt (rhymes with "not")

Mach-pē′lah ("ch" as in "Jericho")
Mah Nish-tä-nah′
Mah Tô′vu
Ma-năs′seh
mä-tzah′
Mĕr′i-bah
me-zu-zah′
Mĭd′i-an
Mĭr′i-am

GLOSSARY

Mō'ab
Mo-rī'ah ("i" as in "ice")
Mō'ses

Năph'ta-lī ("i" as in "ice")
Nē'bō
Něg'ev
Nīle
Nō'ah

Ŏg (rhymes with "log")

Pā'ran
Phā'raōh
Phĭ-lĭs'tĭnes (accent the second syllable)
Pŏt'i-phar
Pu-rim'

Rā'chel
Re-běc'ca
Reu'ben
Rôsh Ha-sha-nah'

Sā'rah
Sā'rai
Sê'der

Shä-vu-ôt'
Shē'chem ("ch" as in "Jericho")
Shmä Yis-rä-ĕl' Ä-dô-nai' Ẽ-lô-hê'nu Ä-dô-nai' Ẽ-chäd
shô-far'
Sĭd-dūr'
Sī'hon ("i" as in "ice")
Sĭm'e-on
Sī'nai
Sŏd'om (the first "o" as in "not")
Suk-kah'
Suk-kôt'
tăb'er-nă-cle ("a" as in "hat")
Tē'rah
Tish-ä' B'Äv
Tō'rah
Tu Bî-shvat'

Ûr (rhymes with "fur")

Yis-rä-ĕl'
Yôm Kip-pur'

Zĕb'u-lun
Zip-pō'rah

#394

Hara
Cyprus
Damascus
Beth-El
Mediterranean
Sea
Jerusalem
Hebron
Goshen
Beersheba
Egypt
Nile River
Red Sea